Very best wr
Dead Engine Kids
John Welch

DEAD ENGINE KIDS

WORLD WAR II DIARY OF JOHN J. BRIOL

B-17 BALL TURRET GUNNER

with

COMMENTS FROM NOTES

OF

OTHER CREW MEMBERS

Silver Wings Aviation, Inc.

2933 Country Club Drive

Rapid City, South Dakota 57702-5218

DEAD ENGINE KIDS

John F. Welch

Editor

ISBN 0-9637909-0-0

Second Printing
October 2001

TABLE OF CONTENTS

FOREWORD

This is an account of long ago events recorded in the words of the participants. The reader should not be surprised to find some discrepancies in the reporting of incidents that happened to all the reporters at the same time. In the heat of combat, each observer saw things differently, from a unique point of view. Each recorded his memories of each mission shortly after it was flown, without being aware that anyone else was keeping such a record. Consequently there was no comparison of notes to achieve agreement on what was written.

Nonetheless, the reader is expected to gain some understanding of the physical, mental and spiritual trauma undergone by the bomber crew members individually and collectively.

DEDICATION

This book is dedicated to the memory of those who gave their lives that the cause of freedom might be advanced, and to those who also served, and survived.

John F. Welch

PROLOGUE

1944 was almost long ago, now, but it was a time of tremendous events, which are still fresh in the minds of many of their participants. Boys became men in the space of a few hours. Some men became heroes, some became casualties, some both, and the lives of all were forever changed.

These things may be said especially of bomber crews. All the members were volunteers, some because they wanted to fly, some for the glamour of it all, some to avoid the walking army, some because flying duty seemed to be a way of contributing.

This book tells the story of one such crew, mostly in the words of the Ball Turret Gunner, John Briol. Combat diaries were forbidden, but his daily written record was the only way he felt he could keep his sanity. And when his tour was over, he sewed it into the lining of his Army field jacket to take it home with him. It came to my attention years after his death, when his grown son sent me a copy. I am both humbled and inspired by it, and scared all over again when I read it.

Lauren Spleth, the crew's First Pilot, kept notes on each mission, which his widow, Rita, generously donated to this project.

Norman Ozenberger recorded the events of some of the missions, as he saw them from his seat as Nose Gunner and Toggalier (Bomb Releaser). My own notes and comments here and there provide another viewpoint and may elaborate on or clarify some of the happenings.

Some mindless system cast us together as a B-17 crew, early in 1944. None of us had ever seen any of the others, but before our association came to an end, we were more closely knit together than any family, having laid our lives on the line for each other on a daily basis. The word was never spoken, but there was a love between each of the men and the other crew members that somehow sustained us through the most terrible days of our lives.

The crew at the beginning included:

Lauren Spleth, First Pilot, from Oklahoma

John Welch, Copilot, from Kansas

Jack Galloway, Navigator, from Florida

Ray Ward, Bombardier, from Missouri

Robert Haynes, Engineer and Top Turret Gunner, from Ohio

Edward Grybos, Radio Operator and Top Gunner, from Pennsylvania

John Briol, Assistant Radio Operator and Ball Turret Gunner, from Minnesota

Norman Ozenberger, Waist Gunner, from Kansas

John Byknish, Waist Gunner, from Ohio

Harry Cornell, Tail Gunner, from Michigan

Spleth, Galloway, Ward, and Ozenberger were married; Galloway had a small son.

We learned to use the B-17 as a crew at Drew Field, Florida, then went to Langley Field, Virginia, where Galloway and Ward learned navigation and bombing by radar, still in its infancy. Finally we loaded our gear and ourselves on a new B-17, equipped with the new radar, called Mickey, and departed for the Eighth Air Force, based in England.

No amount of training, no matter how realistic, ever adequately prepares men for combat. It is under fire that they develop into real fighting men. That was not to take long.

It required a certain mental set to daily risk one's life in aerial combat. It goes something like this: A commander calls in ninety-nine men who have volunteered to go with him on a certain mission, and says,

"This mission we're going on is so dangerous that it's likely that only one of the hundred of us will come back alive."

Every man there looks around and says to himself,

"Those poor guys!"

This was the mental attitude it took to keep on flying bombing missions, scared half to death, but cautiously optimistic. The names and assigned units displayed on the grave markers, and on the Walls of the Missing, in the U. S. Military Cemeteries of Europe, are witnesses to the reality.

John F. Welch
1993

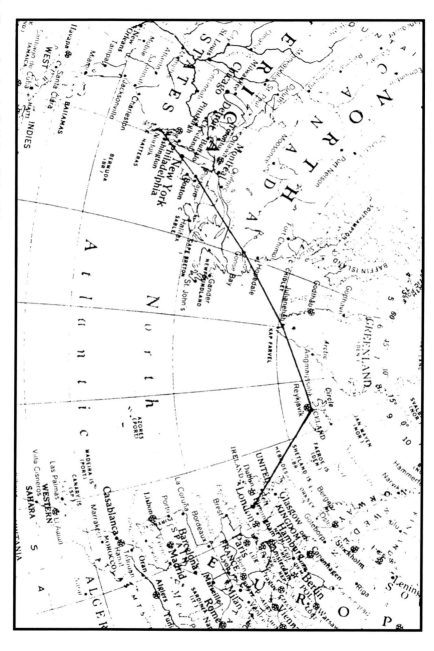

Figure 1. The route from Langley Field, Va. to Valley, Wales

10

CHAPTER I

ON THE WAY TO ENGLAND

Briol, July 27 and 28, 1944

Langley field, Va., alerted for overseas. Took off at 8 A. M. Circled Mitchell Field, N. Y. for instructions. Passed over Brooklyn, N. Y. City. Landed same day at Grenier Field, New Hampshire. Guarding plane. Saw English Mosquito plane on July 28. Ceiling 500 ft. when coming into Grenier. Hard time finding field. Narrowly missed broadcasting tower. Rough weather.

Welch, July 27, 1944

We're not real ready for hard instrument flying. We got too low going toward the range station on final. Thank goodness we missed the "cone of silence". We saw the towers go by, reaching above us, off to one side.

Briol, July 29, 1944

We're sitting around ship waiting for fog to lift. Birds are even walking. Fog came in again, grounded all day. My Buddy and I guarded the airplane starting at 1800. Slept in sleeping bags in ship tonight.

Briol, July 30, 1944

Still bad weather. Went to dance on post tonight.

Briol, July 31, 1944

Took off at 8 A. M. No. 1 engine conked and we had to make an emergency landing. Took off again at 2 P. M. No. 3 engine went out this time. Looks like we'll never get out of this hole. Land is desolate from now on.

Briol, August 1, 1944

Took off at 0815. Just passed into Canada. On our way north-east to Goose Bay, Labrador, flying course of 041 degrees. We've had nothing but small mountains and pine trees below us for five hours now.

Landed at Goose Bay, Labrador this afternoon. Raining, covered engines etc. on ship. Nearest city in Maine almost a half thousand miles away. Hudson Trading Post is about 20 miles.

Briol, August 2, 1944

Nothing to do today except guard ship and wait. Went swimming today with Canadian airmen. Water was very cold. It's always cold here, even in summer. A lot of dogs (husky) around for pulling sleighs. I guess nights are four hours long.

Briol, August 3, 1944

Didn't do anything worth mentioning today.

Briol, August 4, 1944

Briefed at about two o'clock this morning. Takeoff delayed for a while, then called off because of weather.

Briol, August 5, 1944

Still couldn't take off because of weather.

Briol, August 6, 1944

Briefed at four in the morning. Took off 7 A. M. We're out of America on our way to Greenland. We're going to use oxygen to pass over the glaciers of Greenland. Been over water all morning. Flying blind now. Air so rough I can hardly write. Good thing we have de-icers or we'd be loaded with ice.

Just ran into a snow storm. I'm watching the ice form on the wings, but it falls off because of the de-icers.

Over Greenland, I was astonished by the hundreds of icebergs in the water, larger than a battleship, a sight I'll never forget. Mountains rising out of the sea 7,000 ft. high covered with glaciers. Now, we see icebergs that must be almost as big as a city block or larger. Our altitude about 10,000 ft. We're headed for Iceland now.

We spent the afternoon over the ocean again. Quite a few clouds below us, landed at Meeks Field, Iceland, 1900 G.M.T.

Briol, August 7, 1944

Not even trees or grass here, just rocks. Woke up at 3 o'clock this morning. Preflighting ship before taking off for England.

The buildings here are round on top and weighted down because of the high winds. Didn't even get to sleep on a mattress last night.

Took off this morning at about 0800. Had good weather. Sighted British Isles about 1605. Encountered little storms along way. Flew over tip of Ireland. Changed course and went over Scotland down into Wales. Landed in Valley, Wales, about 1800. Slept in British barracks.

Welch, August 7, 1944

We, the flight crew, performed a 25-hour inspection on the airplane before getting on board. Not much to it.

We were met in Valley by a bunch of kids asking, "Got 'ny gum, Chum?"

Briol, August 8, 1944

Boarded train for Stone, England. Getting used to British customs, driving on left side of road, stone fences and buildings, quaint things. Changed our money to pounds, half crowns, shillings, six-pence, etc.

Briol, August 9, 1944

Arrived at Howard Hall in Stone.

Briol, August 10, 1944

Went to town and visited pub, etc.

Figure 2. An aerial view of Glatton Air Field. (U. S. Army Photo)

14

CHAPTER II

PRE-COMBAT TRAINING

Briol, August 11, 1944

Boarded train for Westingsnite, England. Right on Channel, now. We can hear rumbling of guns from here. Rocket bombs come near by.

Briol, August 12 and 13, 1944

Formations of our bombers flying over on way to France and Germany. My turn soon.

Briol, August 14-18, 1944

Living in tents, full of bullet holes. No pillows. British type mattress and blankets, hard as boards. No sheets or pillowcases. Chow is not so good. Got a case of GI's yesterday. A little tea and hovie shop near the place. In school we learn about new German jet propulsion planes attacking formations. They are good for about 15 minutes flight at over 600 M. P. H.

A British Mosquito plane crashed in the Wash nearby. Robot bombs (buzz bombs) are still coming over. They do about 400 M. P. H. when they get here.

The Luftwaffe is still very active, especially over main parts of Germany. Flak is always very heavy.

Welch, Pre-Combat School, Watford, England, August, 1944

We're told in this school that the air war has been won, and we won't see any German fighters in our 25-mission tour.

Everybody gets E & E (Escape and Evasion) pictures to carry along on combat missions. If one were to crash land or bail out, he is supposed to contact the Underground, who will use the pictures to make up false ID cards. Since everybody wears the same shirt, tie and jacket for the pictures, we won't fool German Intelligence for very long.

We were standing in line today waiting to get E & E pictures taken when the air raid alert system (Tannoy, PA system) sounded. Ordinarily it gives out a bit of garbage, then says "Take cover!" This afternoon we heard,

"TAKE (BOO-OO-OOM!!!)---cover." My pants legs fluttered with the concussion. So now we've come under enemy fire.

It was a V-1 "buzz" bomb. We never saw it, but hear it raised heck with a cabbage patch. We saw one going by at low altitude yesterday, a British Mosquito bomber right on its tail. It sounded just like my Grandpa's old Fordson tractor going up the road.

Briol, August 30, 1944

We're operational, now, and flying again. We've moved to the 457th Bomb Group, 748th Bomb Squadron, Air Force Station 130 (Glatton), near Peterborough. We're in huts now. We're occupying the beds of a crew shot down over Germany. There's room for three crews in here. Yesterday a plane made it back to the field here only to crash while landing.

Today our other crew in this hut was shot down over Germany. We have a small radio in here and Fred Allen is on but no one hears him right now. If only people knew. I wonder if we can keep going. If Marcella ever reads this I want her to know I'm thinking of her now.

To change the subject: these air bases are really situated differently than American bases. There's a large space for the landing field and operations buildings, etc. Our huts, tents, etc. are almost situated right in with the civilian homes. England's villages aren't spaced like ours. Villages are all crowded together. England is small but it has a lot of people. From the air the buildings on these bases cannot be told apart from the rest of the village.

By looking at the women you can tell they're different after going through five years of war.

Last week I had all my hair cut off for combat. It's about three quarters of an inch now.

Some time ago a German fighter flew over one of the groups here and strafed a chow line. Sixteen men were killed. We're quite far behind the lines right now but when we fly a mission we'll fly over the lines right smack into the heart of Germany.

16

Another crew is in here to replace the last one. Most of the music on the radios is Scotch, Irish and English, but some of it is American for the soldiers over here in the E.T.O.

When we fly so high it gets as cold as sixty below zero or more. You can't take off your gloves or your fingers will freeze solid and if you'd happen to knock them against something they'd fall off.

The ship we had yesterday is patched all over from flak holes. Although we'll fly at a terrific height the German antiaircraft (flak) guns can shoot their projectiles all the way up to us (4 or 5 miles straight up). They are quite accurate. They've been at it for years. Now and then they get a direct hit. Our speed, height and wind currents throw the projectiles off a lot. These enemy guns on the ground use radar to get our range. We throw out chaff (little metal strips) to mess up the radio (radar) waves.

The German fighters do not always attack the whole formation. They usually pick on one squadron if it is loose and try to break it up to make stragglers.

The radar ships that I trained in at Langley accompany the bombers in bad weather, whenever there are clouds below or the ground is not visible. The Mickey (radar) ships have a radar turret in place of the ball turret. By radio waves the ground is reflected on to a viewplate inside the ship. By looking at the viewplate you can see the ground even though you're in clouds or at night. Something like Buck Rogers.

Flying at these altitudes, it's human torture, on oxygen most of the time, the intense cold, the enemy fighters, the enemy flak. All the missions are long now, flown right to the heart of Germany. We'll fly over France and the fighting lines. It's hard to see the action below at high altitude but sometimes we'll have to come back low, that's when we'll really see things.

I ride the Ball Turret most of the time, a perfect position for strafing. Most fellows are afraid of the ball.

Welch, August 30, 1944

We're back together as a crew, after being separated by specialty for pre-combat training. We're assigned to the 748th Bombardment Squadron, 457th Bombardment Group (Heavy), Air Force Station 130, Glatton, England. We're losing Galloway and Ward. Because of their "Mickey" training at Langley, they're going to Alconbury, and will be sent out from there to fly with Group lead crews. We'll have Ted Braffmann, a bombardier trained to use the G-box. Ozenberger moves from waist to nose, where he will operate the chin turret and drop the bombs when he is told. Braffmann will navigate using the G-box and dead reckoning (D. R). He has already flown some missions.

Most navigation is done by the formation leader. Braffmann will try to keep track of where we are, just in case.

Radio compass is not much good over the continent because the Germans set up stations on our frequencies to confuse us. There aren't any U. S. type Radio Range Stations. Our base has a low power radio compass transmitter, also called a "buncher", on the field. It is used to help assemble formations and for low visibility approaches. A good man on the G-box can bring us in on the end of the runway. We hope Braffmann is good.

All the crew members except the pilots man machine guns for defense when needed.

Briol, September 1-4, 1944

They had a dance for us here at the base tonight. I danced with a couple British women for the first time. (They sure like the Yanks.) I didn't stick around long. Went back and hit the sack. It gets a guy's mind off flak and fighters for a while. A Fortress took off today and a British truck must have been crossing the runway. The pilot pulled up to miss it but the tail dragged through the truck killing the men in the truck. The plane got off the ground okay.

There's an old "castle" (country mansion) not far from here. They use it for injured evacuees and elderly people from the London buzz bombings (robot bombs).

Briol, September 4-6, 1944

We were waiting around last night, sweating it out to see who was on the loading list for the mission today. It was bad weather today so no one flew. We lost our bombardier and navigator to a radar squadron, so one of us enlisted men has to

18

be toggalier. He's the one who will toggle out the bombs instead of the bombardier when we're over the target. We're flying nine man crews now. The toggalier doesn't have to know how to use the bomb sight, because all the ships toggle out their bombs the same time the lead ship does. The lead bombardier does the calculating for the whole group or squadron.

Flak is especially heavy over Berlin and the Ruhr Valley, which is known to the airmen as "Happy Valley". Everyone shudders when they know they have to fly over it.

Briol, September 6-8, 1944

Did some tinkering around with a bike today. I'm an old hand at that sort of thing. I did some washing, too, today. I usually do my own. The civilians will do it quite cheap for you, though.

We've had a lot of rain lately. The water really runs in here. Sometimes at night the rats actually run over your covers.

Briol, September 8-10, 1944

I don't see how those Fortresses can take it. Ours wasn't bad but one crew came in with over 50 holes in their ship made from bullets and flak, leaking gasoline, oil and everything else; one tire was shot off. On the landing they swerved off the runway into the mud and almost sank up to their belly. Another crew was accidentally shot up by another Fortress. Five .50 caliber slugs tore through the wings and bomb bay loaded with block busters. I think about every ship was damaged today. Over the radio they're talking about the big league baseball scores but here we're talking about how lucky our crews were to escape with their lives.

Over the target today the flak was everywhere. It seemed to be miles above, below and around. Some burst so close you'd swear you were a goner for sure.

I hear there were a couple little English fellows back in our hut sweating out the crews. There are a few English boys and girls who straggle around camp as if they were part of it. One fellow was in today (I guess he knows us all by name in this hut) asking if each one was still there or came back again.

I hear there isn't much left of the Luftwaffe but it's not so. There are plenty enemy fighters concentrated in certain spots. You run into them now and then. The flak is deadly enough, not saying anything about fighters. The group bombed Ludwigshafen, Germany, two consecutive missions, on the 3rd and the 9th. I haven't flown any missions to describe in full yet, but I'll get around to it.

People hardly ever hear about the accidents that happen on these missions, not caused by the enemy. For instance, a couple days ago, over the Channel, a chin turret gunner had charged his guns and accidently got a runaway gun. It killed a Ball Turret gunner standing in the waist in the ship ahead and shot a leg off one of the waist gunners. This is only in our own group. We hear very little about what goes on in the other groups. A little more about Ludwigshafen. It was quite a hot spot.

I'm praying we'll never get a direct hit in our bomb bay. There is nothing left when that bomb bay with eight thousand pounds of bombs gets a direct hit.

Welch, September 1-9, 1944

We've been flying some training missions. Some things are different as compared to training in Florida.

Out of Drew Field we flew 18-ship formations. Here we've been introduced to flying in a 12-ship "box". The box consists of four elements of three airplanes each, a lead element, a high right element, a low left element, and a lower element in trail behind the lead element. The position of element lead behind the box leader is called the "slot". This formation allows the box to fly a very tight defensive formation, able to bring thirteen .50 caliber machine guns per airplane, 156 total for the box, to bear on attacks from various quarters. Thank the Lord I'm not a German fighter pilot.

A Group formation is three boxes, leader at nominal altitude, right box high, left box low. The high and low boxes fly a short distance behind the lead box.

On the bombing run, the box formation spreads out a bit into a flattened diamond, so that no element will likely drop bombs on one below it. The box "front" is then about 1,000 feet wide. All aircraft drop their bombs when the box leader drops his. If he is zeroed in on the center of the main target, no bomb should miss it more than 500 feet. This should work well on limited area targets like railroad yards and synthetic oil refineries. (The box leader's first bomb trails smoke).

We've learned that the number 3 position in the low left element of the box is "Tail End Charlie". It's easy to get flung out of position on a box right turn. Because that position is least likely to interfere with other aircraft in the maneuvering of the box, a new crew is just about certain to be assigned to it, and may become a straggler in turn off the target, etc. German fighter pilots like stragglers.

We have been told that each crew gets to go home after 25 missions, and each member is awarded the DFC for completing a tour. Right after we got here, we talked to a crew that had just finished its tour, had been given their DFC's, and are on the way home. They were kind of strutting around with big grins, saying it was easy. I hope so.

Briol, September 10, 1944

I hate to write this stuff. I feel like brooding over it. One way to get it off my chest. The Group flew this morning. One fighter went down in flames. We lost Lafayette today, the fellow who slept right beside me. I think Bob McCann went down too. Lafayette's ship collided with another over France on the way to the target. His tail was chewed off. One man parachuted. Some of the men in our other ships were wounded.

It's a funny thing. Lafayette's whole crew was lost about two weeks ago -- he was saved because he didn't fly with them that day. Now today he flew with another crew and he got it.

Spleth Mission No. 1, September 10, 1944
Target: Gaggenau, Germany

Rode as co-pilot with 1st Lt. Jimmie Scherrod. Had trouble with #3 engine before reaching Target. Finally detonation died down and was able to use engine over target. No fighter opposition. Light but accurate flak. No damage to crew or plane. Bombs away at target. Lead box, #1 high flight.

No flying today except a practice mission later on. When we don't fly for some reason or other we usually have to go to school to keep brushed up on things. It keeps us from thinking of the harmful things. It used to be that you'd fly twenty-five missions and you'd go back to the States but they've changed it. I don't know how many I'll fly.

To tell the truth I don't see how a man can put in as many as 35 and keep from going completely crazy . That is, if he's lucky enough to be alive. All I want to do is finish the job and go back to Marcella.

It's starting to get cold around here. I hate to think of the missions during the winter. There have been some fifty below zero missions in even this weather.

Figure 3. Spleth's Crew - Front row: Harry Cornell,
John Briol, John Byknish, Robert Haynes
Rear row: Norman Ozenberger, John Welch,
Lauren Spleth, Ted Braffmann, Eddie Grybos
(Photo Courtesy Rita Spleth)

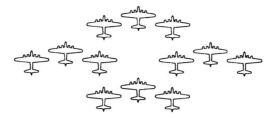

Top View, En Route

Rear View, En Route

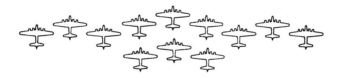

Top View, On Bombing Run

Rear View, On Bombing Run

Figure 4.   Diagrams of B-17 formations, en route
            (above), and on a bombing run (below)
            (John F. Welch)

CHAPTER III

COMBAT!

Briol
Crew Mission No. 1, Group Mission No. 121, September 12, 1944

We had our first mission this morning. My stomach still has a sick feeling and my knees are still wobbly. We bombed Ruhland.

I'll start from the beginning. We got up at two o'clock this morning. It may take me a couple days before I feel like writing about these missions. I don't even like to think about them.

Before we eat breakfast some of us who are Catholic go down before each mission for Absolution and Communion. When we go out to face death we can receive Communion without Confession or we can even eat breakfast before but it's not recommended. I feel much better when I can receive like that. Then we went down to briefing.

They raised the curtain on the map where our route and mission were laid out. All the airmen groaned. We knew a lot of us wouldn't come back. All they did to console us was to say, "It's not pretty," and they let it go at that. The route was marked so we had to fly all the way across Germany to the other side to Ruhland. We had to pass near Berlin on the way. Our target was the Synthetic Oil Refinery at Ruhland. They throw everything at you there, their rocket ships and everything, not to say anything about flak.

After briefing we went to the equipment room where we keep all our flying equipment. We drew parachutes and harness and Mae Wests.

We carry .45 automatic pistols in a shoulder holster. (We keep them with us in the hut.) We use electrically heated clothing, pants, coats, gloves and shoes, oxygen mask, helmet and goggles, flak suits, escape kit containing maps, compass, etc., in case one has to bail out or crash land in enemy territory. When you're in the ship you're a mass of wires. One to your throat mike, one to your headset, one to your electric suit and a hose to your oxygen mask. We get one B-4 bag to a ship which contains one extra thing of everything if something should go out on you. We pile all this stuff outside and then we go to the armor building for our machine guns. Before a mission we have to clean the oil off and check everything. We have to take the oil off or they'll freeze up at high altitude. After a mission we clean them and put the oil back on. We have to install them before every mission.

A truck takes us out to the plane. It has to be preflighted, guns put in, a million things checked. We put on all our equipment and take off. After we're over the Channel we take our positions and pray that we'll see England again.

We usually hit the coast of France, Belgium or Holland. We pass over the lines where we see the boys fighting it out on the ground below. We have to fight it out in the air, over Germany.

After we get into Germany the flak starts coming up at us but it's not so intense until we get to the target. Fighters won't bother us until we get close to the target, unless we're caught straggling along behind our formation.

After hours of sweating it out and praying, we saw Berlin in the distance. It seemed to be smoldering from the pounding we're giving it. We passed near it a little to one side to avoid the intense flak.

Then it happened so quick you couldn't think. We heard the report "Bandits"! They seemed to come from nowhere. The Nazi fighters came barreling through our formations before you could wink an eyelash. I watched terrified as three of our Fortresses went down in flames with their bomb loads and our buddies in them. I saw five men get out of one of them. The rest were lost. One of them kept falling, I never did see his chute open.

By this time I had my guns charged on as one came flashing by our ship. One of our escort fighters was on his tail, pouring lead into him. Besides that, a couple other Fortresses were giving it to him. You could have recognized the pilot if it weren't for his oxygen mask. He must have been dead as he went by.

I think about 54 of our Fortresses and Liberators were lost on this raid. We had one engine gone but we kept up with the formation to the target at Ruhland and left it in flames. We turned around and beat it back across Germany. It wasn't long and another engine quit.

I was never so scared in my life because we didn't have enough power to keep up with the formation. We couldn't keep up with them so we were left straggling across Germany on two engines and losing altitude. When you're all alone like that your greatest fear is enemy fighters ganging up on you. They were getting our range from the ground and the flak would come up and almost knock us down. We lost altitude down to about 10,000 ft. Then the engines seemed to hold us.

God was with us though because we weren't attacked. Every time we saw a speck on the horizon we were terrified. We sweat it out for hours over Germany until we finally passed over the fighting lines into France, the happiest moments of our lives.

We almost headed for Switzerland because it was closer but our engines managed to carry us back over the Channel. Coming back from a mission and seeing the shore of England is the sweetest thing in the world.

Spleth Mission No. 2, Sept. 12, 1944 (Tuesday) (662 X-ray)
Target: Ruhland, Germany

First mission with own crew. #2 engine prop ran away at same time Division was attacked by fighters just East of Berlin. Had trouble keeping formation. Got back into formation and stayed by turning inside of formation on turns. Lost #2 definitely at target. Was drawing about 15 inches Hg. Dropped bombs possibly short of target. Lost formation due to #2 engine, and #3 engine starting to lose oil. Was able to use #3 for about 30 minutes, but had to feather it at about 18,000 ft. Airspeed dropped off to about 100 mph to maintain altitude. Zig-zagged back and forth over Germany to miss flak areas. Finally lost altitude to about 13-14,000 ft. and regained use of #2 engine. Made it back to England O. K.--saw a little flak off to our right as we crossed the French/Belgian coast. Landed with 300 gallons of gasoline left.

We had called for fighter support on "A" Channel, but got none, neither did we encounter any enemy fighters coming across Germany.

All four engines had to be changed--glad to get home.

Not much flak at target.   Ship # 662 X-ray #6 low
squadron.

Ozenberger Mission No. 1

Our first mission on September 12 would have seemed
rough even if it wasn't, just because it was our first one.

The target was Ruhland, Germany. Our briefing time
was 4 A. M. and the target was a synthetic oil plant. Our bomb
load was 5,000 pounds, full gas load.

This being our first mission, we were very green and
didn't know just what we were in for. Everything went well for
us until we got near Berlin, and then the fun began. To tell the
truth I don't know whether I was scared or excited. I think it
was a mixture of the two.

The enemy fighters (Bandits) hit about twenty to thirty
minutes before our target. However, they didn't hit our group.
I saw my first real dog fight over at my left about ten high. I
saw several fighters go down. I wasn't close enough to see if
they were ours or theirs. (By the account in the paper the next
day, I found out that most of the fighters shot down were
theirs). A few of the enemy fighters came past us but didn't
bother us.

Later on, as we flew close to Berlin, a Group of B-17's
off to our right got too close and were broken up by the Berlin
flak, and they came flying through our Group. After shuffling
the deck with us (going through us) they were completely split
up. The Bandits saw their chance and really hit them. I saw a
few of the 17's going down in flames, one that blew up, and
another one going down with one wing gone.

By this time we were on the bomb run. About three
minutes from the target our number two engine went out. That
put us behind and we went on to drop our bombs alone.

We then started home, and our number three engine
went bad on us, although we didn't have to feather it (turn it off
. . . . however, in not feathering it an engine was pretty badly
used up).

I thought there was a lot of flak over the target, but later
I found out that the flak we got on our first raid was light. All
the way back we had to sweat out the fighters, which we thought
would hit us at any time. When we were about half way back

across France, we had to feather our No. 3 engine, due to leaking oil. No. 2 was able to provide some power at the lower altitude.

We got back about an hour late, and everyone on the field thought we had gone down. But here I am and able to talk about it. No one was hurt on the run.

Welch Mission No. 1, September 12, 1944

This first mission for our crew was like seeing a war movie, except that we were wearing flak suits and flak helmets instead of 40-mission crush caps.

The flak suits cover the vital areas of our torsos. They are fabric covered steel strips held in place by horizontal stitching. The pilots have armor plate behind their seats, so wear only the front panels of the flak suits. Other positions wear a back panel also, except for the ball turret, where there just isn't room enough. The suits are supposed to stop relatively low velocity projectiles like shrapnel from exploding artillery shells. They won't stop a .50 caliber bullet. The suits get awful heavy after several hours.

Flak helmets look like those that foot soldiers wear, except that they have hinged flaps over the ear portions of the leather helmet. Ball and top turret wear a leather bound assembly of strips like those in the flak suits, because there isn't room in the turrets they man for a regular flak helmet.

On this first mission the gunners had some problems installing the machine guns, so that we were barely ready to start engines on time. Because we were a new crew, we were assigned the "tail end Charlie" position, number three in the low left element in the 12-ship box. In that position we were least likely to get any other aircraft in trouble.

As we assembled and climbed to our first sustained high altitude flight (26,000 feet for our Group) Ozenberger initiated the oxygen check-in of all crew members every 5 minutes, for the duration of the high altitude flight.

On our way across northern Germany our coming was obviously noted, as evidenced by the generation of smoke screens on the ground, completely obscuring most terrain and cultural features.

The Group following us was assigned 28,000 feet, which

meant that their low box and our high box were at about the same altitude. The tail wind was greater at 28,000, so the following Group began S-ing to keep from over-running us. Just about the time we entered the Berlin area, they turned right again, and picked up heavy flak. They turned left to get out of the flak, so that their low box swept through our high box, breaking up both formations. Our high box quickly reformed, but their low box was scattered all over the sky. The German fighter pilots saw this as an opportunity, and attacked. We were not targeted, probably because our formation was still intact.

I looked off to the right and saw a B-17 going down in flames. Another's tail gunner was trading shot for shot with a fighter coming in behind them. Our crew was so taken with it all that no one even fired a shot.

Our Group did not bomb its assigned target, but another which showed up. The photo interpreters at Glatton have identified it as a large aluminum plant, we found out later at mission debriefing. They also said our crew's bombs fell short.

We lost most of the power from No. 2 engine before we got to the target, and fell back, causing our late bomb release. No. 3 began leaking oil over the target, and we had to feather it a little while later. The reduced power meant we straggled behind, and had to slow down to maintain some altitude. When we got lower, we picked up some power from No. 2, and were better able to hold our own. No. 2's supercharger must have been out.

We landed at least an hour after everyone else, but I don't think we were even reported as missing.

Briol, Wednesday, Sept. 13, 1944
Crew Mission No. 2

Our mission was to Lutzkendorf and one of the marshalling yards. We didn't get to drop our bombs on this target but the rest of the formation did. Something like: yesterday our engines lost power and we had to salvo our bombs before got to the target in order to keep up with the formation. There's one thing we couldn't help, though. I'm afraid we wiped out a whole little German village with that 7,000 pounds of bombs. They had no warning either, we couldn't see where we were dropping them

until they hit.   There were planes in back of us, who had
trouble, too, and were dropping them any old place. After we
got rid of the weight we kept up with the formation. Coming
back, we passed over Dunkirk.

Spleth Mission #3, Sept. 13, 1944 (Wednesday)
Target: Lutzkendorf, Germany

Made an instrument takeoff after having trouble getting
our guns in and getting our engines started, and waiting for
them to pull a B-17 out of the mud--it had run off the runway.
Got into formation O. K.

Lots of contrails this morning, very pretty. About
22,000 ft. went through some contrails and propwash, and started
to lag. Closed cowl flaps, dived plane and managed to get back
into formation. With everything forward we again started losing
out and dropping back. Told bombardier to get rid of 3 bombs
--still couldn't catch up. Dropped 3 more, still no soap. Got rid
of the rest and caught formation by turning inside as formation
turned on to I. P. Stayed with formation rest of trip.

Not too much flak at target. Made the unpardonable
mistake of landing at wrong field. Peeled off on the other side
of Polebrook, made touch and go landing at Polebrook and
came home. What a day!!@*?X**!

No battle damage.   Ship #394, #2 low squadron.

Welch, Mission No. 2, Group Mission No. 122, Sept.13, 1944

We dropped all our bombs, a few at a time, to keep up
in formation, before we got to the target.

For landing, visibility was very poor. We saw another
B-17 on downwind leg heading, fell in behind it, and followed
it to landing. About the time we touched down, we saw a lot of
'17's with Polebrook tail markings, so made a touch-and-go,
continuing straight ahead to the Glatton runway for final landing.

It turns out that the reason for straggling behind the
formation until we had dropped all our bombs was that the air
filters on the engines did not go to the unfiltered position when
we moved the switches to select it at 18,000 feet in the climb.
The indicator lights showed unfiltered, but they were lying to
us. With the filters still in the intake air flow, we were not

getting enough air to the engines.

We have been told to expect to have colds for most of the time we're in England. However the medics are trying a new approach. Each crew member is required to take a sulfa pill every day. And they check us off when we take it. We'll see if it works to prevent colds.

Briol
Thursday, Friday, September 14-15, 1944

Don't have to worry about fighters these two days. We got a 48 hour pass.

I went to London again. I looked the city over mostly. The first morning I was awakened by a robot bomb exploding nearby almost jarring the buildings loose. The second morning three exploded nearby about an hour apart. While there, I visited the House of Commons (Big Ben), the Tower of London, St. Paul's Cathedral, Westminster Abbey, Buckingham Palace; a lot of these places are damaged from bombing. Other places of interest are Picadilly Circus, Trafalgar Square, Rainbow Corner.

When you leave London for another place you have to get the right railway station (there's a lot of them). There are different stations for different parts of England.

At the Tower of London we saw where kings and queens were imprisoned and executed. Drawbridge, moat, armor, walls 18 ft. thick at bottom 14 ft. at top. In Westminster Abbey they have the grave of the unknown soldier and many other graves and monuments.

Sunday, Sept. 17, Group Mission No. 123
Briol Mission No. 3

Today, Sunday, we bombed the Siegfried Line, near Nijmegen. It had to work like clockwork. We had to hit it at a certain time so our ground troops could move in and take over after the bombing. We supported the ground forces. We could see the action taking place below. We blasted tanks, troops, pill boxes and everything. We lost a lot of ships again. Not many bailed out. I saw one man's chute trail behind him like a rag. It wouldn't open.

The best part of our ships came back with over 100 holes in each one. I'm always terrorized but I'm getting so I don't care so much, I guess.

We had to get up at two o'clock again this morning, received Absolution and Communion , ate breakfast, briefed, got our equipment and took off. Since the ground troops were depending on us, we had to destroy the target at any cost. We had to keep going straight to the target whether we died or not. A lot did.

This was the part of the line by Holland. Wave after wave went over it. We passed over Brussels on the way back and we saw British Lancasters also headed for the target. Flak was so thick you could almost get out and walk on it. We lost our lead crew today, piloted by a major; God must certainly be with our crew. As usual we were so tired when we landed that we could hardly walk.

Since I got here the missions are tougher because they're farther and the Germans are almost at their end, and they're using everything as a last resort.

After we land we're always interrogated and there's a Red Cross girl to give us coffee and doughnuts. We always get a shot of whiskey to quiet our nerves. It's really good after something like that. I never thought I'd like England, but when I see its coast coming over the horizon after a hard mission it's a glorious sight.

I hope there's bad weather or something tomorrow so we don't have to fly. I feel like I'm living on borrowed time. Maybe some time I can look back at this writing and see how lucky I was. So far it's all like a bad dream.

I've just found out what our bombing was all about today. It was just announced that air borne troops were landed in the Netherlands. Our bombing was to clear the way for these troops. I guess we did a pretty good job. On the way back today I saw those C-47's towing gliders filled with airborne troops, but I didn't know what for. It won't be long until the Netherlands will be liberated.

The German pilots are either very foolish or very good. Some of them are very brave. They'll come through a formation and they know they'll die. Sometimes they're shot down by our bombers and some times they're blasted to bits by one of our fighters on their tail. The FW-190's usually let go with .30

cal. tracer bullets to see how close they're sighting, then when their sights are lined up they let go with their cannon. The explosions keep creeping up on you.

Sometimes the flak is very accurate. Usually when they get your range there's a straight line of explosions right behind your tail, each explosion gets closer. That's when you're a goner. One guy got trigger happy in a Ball Turret today and almost shot down one of our own bombers again.

When we flew over Holland all the canals must have been opened because it was all covered by water where the Germans flooded it.

Spleth Mission No. 4, Sept. 27, 1944 (Sunday)
Target: Nijmegen, Holland--Near Siegfried line.

Easy trip. Takeoff and assembly O. K.--30 minute delay after assembly. Slight flak as we crossed enemy lines in Holland, dropped bombs O. K. with lead and in formation. Came out of enemy territory by same route as entering. Returned O. K. Two ships missing upon return, lead and deputy. Deputy lead crew returned O. K. (later).

Briol, Monday, Sept. 18, 1944

I guess I got my wish today. We haven't got a mission today but we'll get a practice mission some time today. I actually got to sleep till nine o'clock this morning instead of getting up at two. It felt wonderful.

On our practice mission we flew around in formation over the central part of England. We fake attacks by our own fighters to give us practice in tracking, etc. We practiced formation flying because enemy fighters have a harder time breaking up a tight formation.

I think we're going to make some more attacks on the Siegfried line and help our troops out. I like it better than those missions to the heart of Germany where you're getting shot at all the way across Germany like a clay pigeon. On these short runs to the Siegfried line you're over friendly territory a good part of the time because of our advancing ground troops.

Briol Mission No. 4
Tues.- Wed., Sept. 19-20, Group Mission No. 124, Flown
Sept. 19, 1944

We didn't get back to our base until today. We bombed the marshalling yards of the cities of Soest and Hamm yesterday. It was a long mission but there wasn't much opposition. There's always that terrific tenseness of sweating out fighters and flak, though. We also hit a snow storm coming back. It always does me good to see the target being blasted in flames as we turn around and streak for the channel.

We came back over Holland, Belgium and the North Sea yesterday. I'm always watching what's taking place on the fighting line below us as we pass over. When you're low enough you can see the dust, smoke, troops, trucks, tanks etc. Soon as we're over the lines we can relax a little. When you're over Germany on the bomb run--I can't describe the feeling, but you want to get rid of our bombs and get the heck out of there before they get you. You usually have to fight your way to the target and from it.

As we hit the coast of England, all of England was blanketed over with fog. Our lead ship was ordered to some base in England that was not closed in. Our whole formation flew for a half hour when one of the ships ahead of us had its engines go out and fell back. To avoid hitting him we moved over to one side and lost the rest of the formation in the fog. So we were alone and flew around for hours in the fog trying to find a clearing and a field to land on. Everyone was tired and everything else from the mission. We flew along at 500 ft. off the ground and finally located a British field and landed.

As usual we slept in Limey beds. About two o'clock this morning a robot bomb hit about a half mile from us and almost threw us all out of bed. The alert sounded and we all ran out to the air raid shelter. Two more came over and exploded farther away. They sound like a heavy motor cycle when they go over and they usually blow smoke rings behind them. We couldn't see them well because of the fog. This base was quite close to London.

About three o'clock this afternoon our ship was patched up and we came back to our base. By the way, I met a few of the fellows at that other base that went through gunnery school

35

like me. Quite a few of them (our class) were shot down, I found out.

We got our usual shot of whiskey over there. It usually hits me pretty hard on an empty stomach and I had a few extra ones, so did the other guys and combat was forgotten while we had some fun.

I think Ozzie and I are going over to Sawtry tonight. It's a little town about two miles from the base here. We went once before on our bikes and just rode around town until the pubs opened. Then we went in and drowned our sorrows with some English beer. Their beers are called Mild, Bitter and Ale. It isn't as good as ours but it's stronger.

Of course it's their business, but around England you see English women out with Negroes. I don't think much of it myself. You see some strange things here in England, but I've found out it's a strange world.

So far I'm still riding the Ball Turret. I think the rest of the men usually admire the Ball Turret gunner because there are few men who will ride the Ball. It's good that I'm a small man because a large man won't fit so good. I can't wear a chute in it because there's no room. I can't wear a flak suit or helmet. I have my chute harness on and my chute just outside the Ball in the waist. In an emergency I'd have to point the guns straight down, open the door of the turret, climb into the waist, snap my chute on and go out the waist door. The only thing I can do is "Trust in God". When you're in the Ball you're cramped up quite a bit, with your oxygen mask, heated suit, helmet, harness and lots of wires. You're hanging below the belly of the ship and you're the loneliest guy in the world. It seems I am in a metal and glass ball five miles above the earth all alone. You can see all the action from that position.

You can see all the flak coming up at you, you can see all the bombs hit, and when flak hits your turret, you're scared sick even if it doesn't touch you yourself. You have to be spinning around and going up and down all the time while your ship is going almost 200 miles an hour. That alone would make a lot of guys sick.

I had aerobatic flying when in the cadets. I think that helps. I've never been airsick. Our radio operator gets sick almost every mission.

There are some things I like about the ball. It's got a lot of fire power and it has more range than the fighters. Two .50 caliber machine guns right along your hips and you have the 3,000 dollar Sperry computing sight to sight with. Sometimes in the Ball it feels as if you're going over Niagara Falls in a barrel.

It's also the coldest position in the ship but I'm usually quite comfortable with my electrically heated suit. Without that suit I'd be an ice cube in a couple minutes at an altitude of five miles straight up.

These vapor trails that the planes leave behind them at high altitude are really something to talk about. They stream out for miles behind your exhaust. It's like a world of terror you've never known before. I'll admit the men on the ground have it tougher sometimes but there's a lot who wouldn't trade with us, especially after going on one mission and seeing what it's like.

I'm kind of afraid we're due for some missions to Berlin again. I'm deathly afraid of any that even take us within the vicinity of Berlin. I can feel that cold sweat now and my lips quivering every time some one calls out fighters. (I don't know why I write this stuff. I've been on the verge of tearing this up and throwing it away about three or four times.)

It's funny but no matter how scared we are every time we go into combat, we still feel like we're bound in conscience or something to do the job. Still, when it's foggy and bad weather we're all happy that we don't have to go.

The new jet propulsion German fighters are going to give us trouble. There are three to worry about: the HE 180, the ME 262 and the ME 163. The newer ones will easily do over 600 miles per hour. The U. S. is also starting to produce jet propulsion ships. About the only way to combat these ships is with other jet propulsion ships.

I wish we'd get some shuttle runs. On a shuttle run they bomb a target in Germany and go on over to Russia and land. On our missions so far we've been so close to Russia that it would have been much easier to land there instead of coming all the way back over Germany. It would also count as two missions (shuttle) because we'd bomb a target going over and then another when we'd return here to our home base.

Maybe I'm writing this stuff because I'm getting so batty I talk to myself and put it down on paper. On my first missions the war seemed kind of impersonal. I didn't feel sore at the Germans, so to speak. I remember on one of my first missions when we were attacked by fighters I didn't feel like fighting but it was either they or we. For a few minutes in the Ball Turret I felt to hell with the war, the fighters, the bombs and the target and everyone else. I wanted to get out of that ship and the sky and get my two feet on solid ground again, whether it was enemy or not. I got over that feeling. Now that I've been in combat oftener and I've seen what they to to our pals, I'll stick to it and kill every German I get the chance to.

Spleth, Mission No. 5, Sept . 19, 1944 (Tuesday)

Easy mission. Climbed through overcast at 4500 ft. Assembled at Briefed +4, just above clouds. Climbed on course to I. P. Bombed from 24,200. Formation in clouds and contrails at bombs away. Evasive action back to friendly territory.

Bombs away at target O. K. 100%. Not all boxes dropped. Received diversion message on return. Let down through undercast, lost formation in pattern--was cut out. Proceeded to Glatton, but (it) was socked in too tight. Radio compass heading to Bassingborn, 91st, and landed.

Stayed all night in Kneesworth Hall. Had engine repaired, left at 1515 and arrived at Glatton 1530, poor visibility.

Welch, Friday , September 22, 1944

Our standard indicated airspeed in formation is 150 miles per hour, and our normal altitude on the high altitude portion of a mission is 26,000 to 28,000 feet. The true airspeed is about 220 miles per hour.

The B-24's can't fly good formation above about 24,000, and have to indicate at least 160 miles per hour to hold good formation there or lower. That gives them about the same true airspeed as we get, but they're more vulnerable to flak because they're lower. On the other hand, their Pratt and Whitney engines are tougher than our Wright 1200's. We use the same electronic controlled superchargers, and they can safely pull about two more inches of manifold pressure for take off than we can, 48 inches for them versus 46 inches for us.

Our third mission, to Nijmegen, was the only one we've

flown at lower than 24,000; it was at 18,000. We lost our Squadron Commander, Major Hozier, who was flying Group Lead position that day. We like the higher altitudes better. If the new B-29 can go higher than 28,000, we'd like that better yet.

Briol, Saturday, Sept. 23, 1944

We were supposed to fly a mission today, but we were called back before we got to the fighting lines. I don't know why, exactly. For all I know maybe we were flying into a trap or something. We spent the rest of the day fixing on our bikes. I can't explain it, but after taking chances in the air we seem to be kind of reckless on these bikes, kidding around with them or something. We can hardly go to the mess hall without guys running into each other or something. The mess hall is quite a ways from our hut.

We signed up for our ration tickets again, too. We get only two razor blades, a couple candy bars, bar of soap, and seven packs of cigarettes a week (for a while none). We have to shave because if we don't, our oxygen masks will leak at high altitude.

We found a little stove today and fixed it up in our hut. Makes it a little more comfy around here. Lilly Ann Carol is singing "I'll Walk Alone" on our little radio. Man, oh, man, that song gets me. When that song comes on everybody drops everything.

While I'm on the subject of heat, this is what I wear when flying. Over my heavy underwear I wear fatigues. After we're ready to take off, I take off my G. I. shoes and put on my heated (electrically) shoes (felt), over that we wear big heavy felt British boots. Then we put on our electric suit pants and coat. This is plugged together by wires to our shoes and gloves to make contact. We wear heavy socks, too. We put on a pair of thin silk gloves and our heated gloves over them. The silk gloves are used because at high altitude if we ever have to take off our heated gloves for a few seconds, our hands won't freeze so quick or they won't stick to any cold metal if we come in contact with it. We put on our helmets and goggles, with headphones in the helmets, then our oxygen masks with built in microphones. Then our Mae Wests and over that our parachute harness, ready to put on our chutes.

The other guys that don't fly the Ball, put on a flak suit and helmet over everything else. It weighs about 30 lbs.

In one pocket over my heart I carry my prayer book with the metal armor cover. It would stop a light piece of flak. In that pocket I also carry nine photographs taken in civilian clothes to forge passports, etc. if forced down, and a language card.

In one of my front hip pockets I carry a couple tools I made myself in case I ever have to work on my guns in an emergency. In the other pocket I carry a pouch with French money in it and a case containing an escape kit (maps, compass, matches, rations, etc.). I never carry anything in my back pockets, because I found out your hips get plenty sore if you sit on something hard for hours. I wear my .45 pistol under my left arm, it would also stop a small piece of flak.

One of the boys who bailed out from this group (before I came here) came back today. He bailed out right over the fighting lines. He lay in a fox hole scared stiff. Shells, fighting and everything was taking place around him. I think the Germans got him first, because he was a German prisoner.

By the way, if you're not killed when you bail out over German territory, you're taken to Dulag Luft or Stalag Luft, a special place for airmen, for interrogation.

You see the most fantastic things five miles above the earth when you're over the target. You see bombs dropping from your ship and all the ships around you. Flak is bursting everywhere, perforating your ship and bouncing it all over. If ships are hit directly by flak, they'll blow up or go twisting down leaving a trail of black smoke behind them. The same thing happens in a fighter attack. You look down and see your bombs flashing as they explode, knocking the city or target sky high. By the time you've turned around and headed back, all you can see is flame, smoke and dust.

You look back and you can usually see some stragglers (as happened to us a couple times) but there's nothing you can do. When you look back over the target as you leave it, it's all smokey and hazy from all the flak bursts sent up at you. You can still see the pillar of smoke going down to the target for a long time. (Ed. Note - from the leader's first bomb.)

It would be awfully hard not to have a Catholic Priest

here at the base. We're very fortunate to be able to receive Absolution and Communion before every mission. If I'd go on a mission without it, I have a feeling I wouldn't come back.

Monday, Sept. 25, Group Mission No. 125
Briol Mission No. 5

We bombed Frankfurt today. We were supposed to destroy the marshalling yards but we destroyed a lot of the city, too. As usual we got up about two o'clock this morning, received and went to briefing; got our equipment, etc., and went out to the ship. This morning it took us a long time to form over England.

We didn't get back till tonight. Each ship carried twelve 500 lb. bombs. Flak was thick and heavy. Our chaff threw it off quite a bit. We had a bunch of flak pieces still in the ship when it landed. It seems the ground crew always gets them first, but I'll have some souvenirs yet. We didn't drop our bombs on the first run over the target; we had to make a 360 degree circle and go over it again.

I thought they'd have our range for sure this time and blast us, but like before we made it. They had a couple hundred guns around this target and they were pretty accurate. If there's anything that scares you, it's to go through a heavy barrage of gunfire and then make a 360 and go through it again. We blasted the target and pulled out for home.

About 15 minutes from the target the warning, "Bandits in the vicinity", came over the V. H. F. radio. I was so scared I couldn't find my selector switches for a few seconds but I was ready for them. They didn't hit our own group, but I saw one of our Fortresses fall with its tail shot off. No one bailed out. It's not so bad seeing a Fortress fall when everyone gets out, but when they don't get out it's a different story.

I'm always prepared for figthters. I have my guns charged and everything even before I'm over the Channel. All I have to do then is flip my gun selector switches and of course, track, frame and use the trigger switches, which comes natural from force of habit. Our escort fighters had left us to intercept the enemy behind us, but a few of them got through to us. I may know later how many of our ships were lost. (9 bombers, 3 fighters).

Spleth Mission No. 6, Sept 25, 1944, (Monday) (591 W)
Target: Frankfurt, Germany

Early briefing--flew #5 position, low squadron, high box. I believe (an) easy mission--no battle damage. Made four approaches to field before we could get in. Was getting low on gas, as we (had) made a 360 at the target.

Came home with formation.

Welch, Mission No. 5, Sept. 25, 1944

We've been flying a different airplane every mission. Today we flew 591 W, officially known as 591 William. The 748th Squadron's call sign is Wedon. So when we call the tower we'll tell them we're Wedon's War Weary Willie, because this now our assigned airplane.

There are supposed to be 15 crews per squadron, but we're below strength. That has meant that we've flown every mission of the Group beginning with our first mission. With the manning shortage, the number of missions before going home has been increased to 30. We're not happy about it.

The enlisted members of the crew will soon all be promoted to at least Staff Sergeant, as some kind of pay for being shot at. With five missions to his credit, Spleth, as first pilot, is eligible for promotion to First Lieutenant. I should make it if I survive twenty missions, the requirement for copilots.

The whole crew is getting tired and maybe a little jumpy. The early morning briefings and the long hours in flak suits and on oxygen are wearing.

These beds are really something, and don't help much in getting a good n ight's sleep. The mattress is in three pieces, squares about four inches thick. The bed is a regular Army steel cot. We don't have sheets, just OD wool blankets. I usually wake up with my posterior sagging between two of the "biscuits" as we call them.

Our Nissen hut is right next to the one where our gunners live. The builders didn't have enough mortar. The wind blows right through the brick end walls.

Over the door of our gunners' hut is a sign: "Through these portals pass the World's tiredest Mortals.

We bombed Osnabruck today. Our losses were pretty heavy. We were in the lead box. It was a box of twelve ships. When we hit the English coast again, there were seven ships left in the box. Our ship was the only one left in our element. We were hit by flak ourselves. One piece went right through the bomb bay. The flak was intense over the target. Some of it grazed off my Ball Turret, missing the window by my head by inches. We didn't have to get up so early this morning, but we were over Germany practically all day again.

We received, ate breakfast, briefed and got off the ground about 8 o'clock. Each ship carried six bombs, each bomb weighed 1,000 lbs. Imagine what they do when they hit. Today on the last bomb in the rack I wrote, "To Adolph from Marcella", on its tail.

Going over we took the route over the North Sea, then over the Netherlands and the Zuider Zee into Germany. The flak knocked heck out of us. A couple of ships from our box were lost here. As we left the target and left the marshalling yards in ruin, another group in back of us were going over the target. I saw one flaming Fortress fall out of that group. We beat our way back to the Netherlands again. Everyone thought they were safe now; they all took their flak suits and everything off. The worst part of it was, we had dropped down to about 12,000 ft., which put us in range of flak guns. Just as we came to the coast of Holland, they let go with their anti-aircraft guns. The bursts crept up on us from behind.

I just happened to swing my turret around in time to see ship 079 flying right next to us on our left wing, flown by Lt. Gooch, get it. They got a direct hit which went through the bottom, middle of the ship, blew the nose off and sent the upper turret, guns and all, almost into our ship. I think everyone was dead, but the funny part of it was, the ship itself didn't fall right away or burst into flame. It slid out of formation, made a 90 degree turn by itself and lost altitude into the clouds below.

Captain Dupont, the Navigator in the lead plane in our box, was killed by a burst of flak near the nose. We didn't know it right away, but we heard them call the field over VHF to have the ambulance there. Later on we saw the ambulance by the ship when they carried him out. I couldn't recognize him.

We passed up a lot of stragglers today, some of them throwing everything out of their ships to lighten them, so they could stay in the air; ammunition, guns, equipment, clothes, everything.

I hope we don't fly tomorrow, I'm still too shaky. So far we've been flying almost every day or every other day. When we do fly, it's just about the whole day over Germany. Not much sleep at night.

We always miss out on our meals when we're on a mission. I'm losing weight. When we do sleep at night everybody talks in his sleep. I guess I do myself. You can hear "Fighters coming in at six o'clock high," or "Flak at twelve o'clock level". I couldn't sleep so good last night. I was listening to the rats chewing away in the hut here. The blasted things ate my candy bars, too--and they're rationed. Oh yes, I got the Air Medal today. I almost forgot about that.

Spleth Mission No. 7, Sept. 26, 1944 (Tuesday) (591 W)
Target: Osnabruck , Germany

Briefed rather late. Went in backwards to way we were briefed. Bombs away first time. Heavy flak--no fighter opposition. Route took us over Zuider Zee, encountered flak at Holland coast. Some of the ships in our box were hit.

We were flying high squadron #2 lead box. Led squadron part way back. Peeled off and landed with no trouble. Had our first flak holes in bomb bay and one each trailing edge of right and left wings.

Welch, Sept. 26, 1944

The way we get the Air Medal is pretty simple. A notice appears on the Squadron Bulletin Board, announcing,

"The following men have been awarded the Air Medal (OLC). Pick them up in the orderly room."

Each crew member is awarded the Air Medal after flying five missions. After that he is given a bronze Oak Leaf Cluster for it for each additional five missions.

Briol, Wednesday, Sept. 27, 1944. Group flew its Mission No. 127. Spleth's crew stood down.

Happy day, we didn't fly today, I slept till nine o'clock this morning. It's pretty bad weather out anyway. I never before saw the day that I'd love bad weather. Some of our boys did get a mission this morning, though.

This afternoon we have school. I think we get a prisoner of war lecture. If we're ever forced down in Germany, now, and live and fall into civilian hands, they'll murder us. If we're caught by enemy troops, it's not so bad.

There's going to be a Catholic Priest in our little theater tonight at five o'clock to say Mass and a Novena. It's going to be for the people back home praying for us. I'm offering mine for Marcella and my folks. Their prayers have pulled us through when things looked mighty dark. Four of our crew members receive before every mission now. Our right waist gunner was a fallen away Catholic. Now he's better than any of us. He's converted for good. About a week ago he went to Confession for the first time in years, I guess. He was scared but he went through with it.

This morning an engineer walked into a spinning propeller down on the line and got his head cut off.

I've got some more fixing to do on my bike when I get the chance. I've got some clothes to wash, too. It takes me only a few seconds every day to jot this stuff down. I should write more letters but it takes me much longer to write letters, censoring, etc.

It's so blasted hard to write this stuff. I have to force myself to do it. I write about a mission and all the time I know I'll probably see a worse and bloodier one tomorrow. When we're about half through, those that are left get a flak leave to rest up. Man, oh, man, how I could use mine now.

Archie was in again today. (The little English boy I mentioned before.) He brought his little brother with him.

We haven't too much to look forward to. If we finish here, we'll probably have to go to the South Pacific. I'll go nuts if I keep thinking. Home and Marcella seem so far away right now. Our engineer/top turret gunner is getting into bed right now. I can still see him cranking those bomb bay doors by hand on the last two bomb runs. These bombay doors always freeze up at high altitude and they won't come up electrically. Just so we won't have to crank up the landing gear by hand.

Our last two missions it was 50 below at high altitude. I had my heated suit turned up all the way and I was still freezing to death. I don't know what we'd do without these electrically heated suits.

Cologne was bombed today but as I said before we didn't go on that one. On our last mission I hugged that sight for dear life to protect my face and head from flak. I never knew I could make myself so small with one hand on the door ready to get out and one hand on the switches waiting for fighters. When the flak bursts near you, you can even hear it above the roar of the engines and with your ears covered by helmet and earphones. It makes a "whu-ump, whu-ump," sound.

Welch, Sept. 27, 1944

We've become friends with some kids from the village our base is in, Conington. They come around and ask if their Mums can do our laundry. They don't charge much, but we have to furnish the soap. I guess the English folks can't buy soap, shortage due to the war.

I feel complimented--the kids call me "Smiler".

Because there's a good possibility of losing loose-fitting foot gear in a bailout, I tie my GI shoes to my parachute harness before take off, so I'll have shoes to walk around in if I have to arrive at the ground separately from the airplane.

For convenience and ease of moving around in the airplane, some of the crew members use chest type parachutes. Spleth and I wear back packs, remembering a man who was blown from the airplane and survived because he was wearing a back pack.

CHAPTER IV

WE'VE HAD IT!

Briol
Crew Mission No. 7, Group Mission 128, Sept. 28, 1944

Today, as the British would say, "We had it." Again, we were the only one ship of our element of three to return alive. Our squadron only put up 12 ships today (part of another squadron). Only two came back. We were in a box of 12 ships. We bombed the Krupp Works of Magdeburg. Waves of twenty enemy fighters attacked our box of 12 ships. There were a couple hundred enemy fighters in the area. I never expected the Luftwaffe to come back but it did, as I've seen with my own eyes.

I also know that God is definitely with our crew. I'm pretty sure I got a fighter today. I claimed it but I don't think I'll get credit for it because I didn't actually see it fall; I was too busy. I think Ozzie, our toggalier, got one too.

We got up about three o'clock this morning. Got our pass to briefing, went down to the theater, received Communion and went to breakfast.

I've never seen such a nice priest in my life. He's so concerned about the men. He keeps a list of all the men that are lost and also compares the names with those that receive before every mission. He asks us how the missions are, etc.

At the briefing as usual we groaned. This target was right next to Berlin. We were over Germany from early this morning till six tonight. We met some flak on the way to the target but it wasn't so bad, the worst was to come.

As we got to the I. P. we opened the bomb bay doors. We were 40 miles from the target. We had five bombs, each weighting 1000 lbs. We had about 30 miles to the target when we sighted the enemy off in the distance at 3 o'clock level. It's impossible to describe the feeling. There seemed to be hundreds of them. They went around in back of us to 7 o'clock. Then they seemed to break into groups of 20. I don't know where our fighter escort was. They came for us low. I thought we were all lost but we responded automatically. I guess I was fighting like a cornered rat but somehow I wasn't thinking of myself. There were so many I didn't know which one to shoot at. I got my sight on the nearest one and blasted away at him. All of his guns were firing at us. I tracked him all the way up along side our ship still blasting away. I forgot all about short bursts.

As he came alongside, the German Crosses were plain as day. I saw fire and smoke starting to come out the right side of his engine. I may get credit for shooting down that fighter. Our Navigator verified it. He saw it fall in flames. I could see the dead pilot. His oxygen mask was torn off. The ship looked as if it were hanging in the air for a second, then I turned my guns away from him onto another ship just coming up on our tail. My left gun went out but all this time I was still blasting away with my right one. The other plane went off to the left without attacking. There was another going under. I tracked him all across the sky underneath getting in a few shots but he was pretty far away.

The whole ship was vibrating from everyone shooting. I was too busy but I saw most of our planes blazing and burning alongside of us. Farther back I saw one blazing Fortress spinning down and breaking up. I only got in a glance at that.

All of a sudden our fighter escort was there and the enemy planes scattered with P-51's on their tails. That was really a show to see the FW-190's get it instead of our Fortresses. Our interphone had gone out on us and we could hardly talk to each other. These Fortresses are like a flying tomb without an interphone. Our No. 2 engine was shot up from the bandits but it was still pumping away. We made it to the target with the two ships we had left. Our formations were all broken up. Planes were scattered all over. We got our bombs away in the middle of the flak. At first only two bombs went, so we salvoed the other three in time to hit part of the city anyway.

Again our bomb bay doors wouldn't come up, so Haynes, our engineer, had to start cranking again. These doors hold the ship back a lot when open. In the process he busted the hose on his mask and almost passed out from the rarified air. He was trying to hold his breath while some one dug out the extra mask we bring along. His face was starting to get purple and we couldn't leave our positions. The navigator came back and helped him.

Before the fighting started I was in misery because I

couldn't leave the turret to relieve myself. When the fighting started I had worse to worry about, so I didn't notice it again until we were headed for friendly territory. Another thing-- from being in one position all the time my legs and back ache to beat the dickens.

Our whole squadron (box) was shot down, except the two of us.

Spleth Mission No. 8, Sept. 28, 1944, (Thursday) (591 W)
Target: Madgeburg, Germany

Assembled at briefed +2. Proceeded into Germany--#2 detonating, making it necessary to keep manifold pressure down. Hit by flak and fighters at I. P. All boys fired on fighters-- Ozzie claims to have downed one FW. Had turbo shot out.

Was flying #2 low squadron low box, saw rest of element either crippled or shot down.

Bomb bays would not close again after bombs away. Managed to keep up with formation by diving ship. Came back with formation. Only 4 of us left out of a 12-ship box. I flew #4, some fun. Made a poor landing.

Found #2 turbo had been hit hard. Several buckets missing. A bullet (possibly 50 Cal.) entered top of #2 nacelle and came out at bottom. Small hole in left wing.

Lockwall went down, also Schultz, Gamboa and another. We were the only ship in the low element to return.

Ozenberger No. 7, Sept. 28, 1944

A mission that we had trouble with was to Magdeburg, Germany. It was our seventh mission, made on the 28th of September. Flak over the target was bad, but it didn't bother us much--it was the Bandits that had us going.

All went well till we had turned into the bomb run. We had gone down the bomb run some two or three minutes when enemy fighters were seen out at five o'clock. They went out to seven low strung out into a long line and came in at us. Because I was in the nose I didn't see them coming. (I was told over the interphone by those that saw them coming). The first I knew that they had come into range was when Haynes' upper turret went off, and I saw the Jerry's 20 mm's busting in front of us.

That brought me up to my senses.

In a little while a Fockewulf 190 came over our left wing, but I didn't get a shot at him. Another one came right after it and did a stall about 100 yards out in front of us. I started shooting at him and didn't take my finger off the trigger until I knew I had gotten him. I saw pieces fling away from around the cockpit, and parts of the wings and fuselage came off. It caught on fire just before it went into the clouds. I have a feeling that he won't come up and bother us again. I shot at another 190 but missed him.

About this time a group of P-51's came in and finished off or chased off the 190's and 109's. All this happened on the bomb run. We got a few holes from flak and one slug in our number two engine.

After it was all over with we couldn't find any other planes around that we had been flying with, so we went up and joined the lead group.

We didn't know how well off we were until we got back to our base and learned that we were the only plane to get away from the fighters out of the low box (12 planes). One plane was forced down and came back about a week later, but the other ten planes were lost.

I found out after we got down on the ground that Briol (lower ball turret) got a fighter, too. That made two enemy fighters to our credit. We came back on time with three and a half engines. Our No. 2 was damaged a little.

Welch, Mission No. 7, September 28

At mission briefing this morning, we were told of an apparently new tactic by the German fighters, a mass tail attack on a single bomber box by 50 or 60 fighters in line abreast. They wiped out a complete box of B-24's yesterday.

(Ed. note: The 445th Bomb Group lost 25 out of 35 B-24's to enemy fighters on September 27, 1944.)

I was tasked with communications with our supporting P-51's. They were to be in three increments, those flying with us on the way in, those covering us over the target, and some more along the withdrawal route. I was on fighter frequency, and Spleth answered for me on the oxygen checks, because I couldn't both listen on the interphone and talk to the fighters.

50

The leader of the first wave of our fighters picked us up before enemy territory, and they covered us almost to the I. P. He checked out saying the next wave would be along very shortly. I tried contacting them, calling several times without success.

Suddenly I began seeing small white bursts out in front of us. I thought, that's sure funny flak. All at once the top turret cut loose, shaking the whole airplane. Fighters! Those white puffs were 20 mm shells, fuzed to detonate at maximum range if they hadn't hit anything.

I grabbed the control wheel, overpowering Spleth's elevator inputs, and began a series of limited pitching maneuvers. I yelled on the radio that we were under fighter attack, then switched to interphone. Cornell and Briol were reporting a wide line of fighters coming in abeam each other from behind us. Tail, waist and ball were firing frequent bursts. Haynes, in the top turret, said his sight light had gone out, but he kept shooting anyway. Ozzie, up in the nose, kept trying to see something to shoot at.

Then he got his chance. One of the prettiest airplanes I have ever seen in flight, an FW-190, passed us on our left side, going forward. Ozzie swung his turret broadside, and forgot all about short bursts. The fighter rolled left to break away, but Ozzie nailed him. Those twin 50's tore huge chunks from the airplane, and it fell from my view. I know Ozzie got him.

All of a sudden, the P-51's arrived, and the attackers fled. But when we looked around, there were only four of the 12 B-17's still in formation. Our Number 2 engine was putting out very little power, but otherwise we seemed O. K. A B-17 with tail markings from another Group joined with us, but finally left when we crossed the English coast. The rest of the mission was sort of anti-climactic, but we were dead tired. We didn't have much appetite for supper.

Everybody confessed to having prayed pretty hard back there.

Certainly the most powerful and effective prayer I know is the last part of the Ave Maria:

"Holy Mary, Mother of God, pray for us sinners, now and at the hour of our death. Amen."

I have frequently been convinced during these bombing missions that the two events, "now" and "the hour of our death"

Figure 5. 457th Bomb Group in loose formation en route to bomb the Thrid Reich. In front, second from the bottom, is Wedon's War Weary Willie, 591 W, flown by Spleth's Crew on 13 missions. (U.S. Army Photo)

52

were coinciding. The fact that they haven't persuades me of the power of the prayer.

Briol, Friday, Sept. 29,. 1944

Our Squadron and Group couldn't fly today; too many ships and crews shot up. We have to get more new ships and crews. I slept till nine o'clock again this morning. We lost another man out of this hut and the ground crew supply men came in to collect all his clothes and stuff; they were whistling. I could have beat their brains out.

When we landed yesterday one ground crewman walked through the ship. Later he said, "Oh, I didn't know you men had to fire." It wasn't obvious enough with the smoking guns, spent cartridges and links laying all over the ship. I respect the ground crew and everything. Our ship wouldn't stay in the air without them, but they don't realize what you go through up there.

We've got the Presidential Unit Citation. I may get a cluster for downing that enemy fighter.

Welch, Friday, Sept. 29, 1944

The B-17 is a good airplane for flying the kind of formation we use in combat. The throttles are provided with three grips, one on top for outboards, center for all four at once, and lower grips for Nos. 2 and 3. Most of the time, once in formation, the position can be held using only 1 and 4. Spleth and I spell each other off in formation en route, each flying the airplane for ten to fifteen minutes at a time. The man not flying the airplane works with the prop, mixture, rpm and turbo-charger controls to keep adequate power for holding position, while maintaining most economical operation, and monitoring instruments to assure the best possible engine health. If an engine develops a problem, he picks it up immediately, and if necessary takes over the throttle of the affected engine to deal with the problem.

Over the I. P. for a bomb run, Spleth takes over flying the airplane, and I handle everything else. Yesterday it was purely by impulse that I grabbed the wheel and started pitching up and down within a narrow envelope. We think we threw the attacker's aim off just enough to avoid being shot down. We may have spoiled the aim of our gunners a little bit , too.

Briol
Crew Mission No. 8, Group Mission No. 129, Sept. 30, 1944

We helped the ground troops in Holland again today, we bombed Munster. We used some incendiary bombs. Bomb load 5,000 lbs. for each ship, 2300 gallons of gas for each ship. I don't know what was wrong with me today. Fighters didn't hit us for a change but I was the most nervous and jittery since my first mission. I can truthfully say it's much more horrible to see men die in the air than on the ground. I don't ever want my brother Eddie to enlist, especially if it's something like I'm doing.

Our tail gunner (Harry) narrowly missed death today. There was a lot of flak over the target. I think our whole box of twelve ships got through today without a death or a ship lost. While we were on the bomb run before we got to the target, I was watching the group ahead of us as they went over the target. They headed straight on to the target through the flak. I took time off from watching for fighters until they dropped their bombs. One Fortress was hit before their bombs were away. It fell apart. I saw the Ball Turret fall away from the ship with the gunner still in it. You can't wear a chute in the ball. That especially hurts me, because I ride the ball. I often imagine myself falling away from the ship trapped inside the ball without a parachute, five miles down.

I saw one other ship fall. It didn't fall apart or burn. It just headed straight down like an arrow, not even spinning. I saw two men parachute . I think it was a waist and tail gunner. I turned away before the Fortress hit the clouds. I just couldn't look any more. I was actually sick.

I was thinking, we're next, we have to get it sometime but then I thought: I mustn't think like that, because God will pull us through. In the distance I saw the enemy fighters but our escort got them first this time. They didn't get through to us.

At first I thought our P-51's were playing games until I saw one speck smoking disappear into the clouds. Then I knew they were fighting it out. They were at 8 o'clock about 3000 feet below us.

I was afraid of jet propulsion ships today. There was a

Figure 6. B-17 Ball Turret, computer aimed, two .50 caliber machine guns. (John F. Welch)

55

Figure 7. B-17 Chin Turret, two direct sighted .50 caliber machine guns. (John F. Welch)

56

Figure 8. B-17 Left Waist Gun, Hand aimed, one .50 caliber machine gun. (John F. Welch)

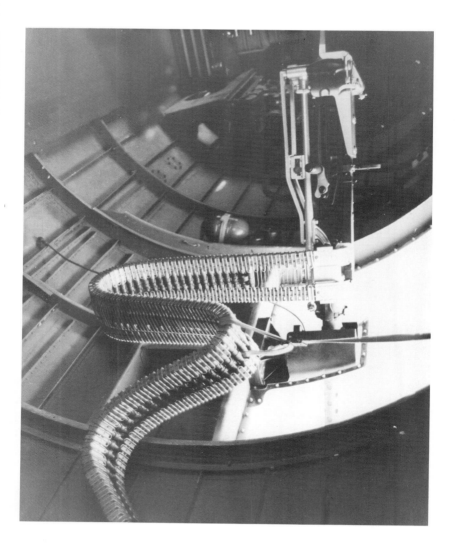

Figure 9.   Internal view, B-17 Right Waist Gun. (John F. Welch)

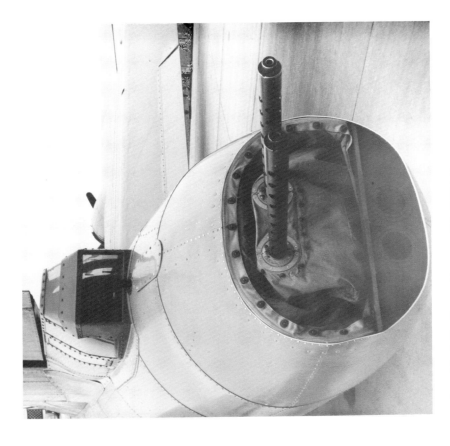

Figure 10. B-17F Tail Turret, two direct sighted .50 caliber machine guns. (John F. Welch)

German air field of them below us. They can easily out run our fighters but they aren't made for long flights.

We got our bombs away and over the target, our tail gunner almost got it but we made it.

Now I'm getting so I sweat out ordinary take offs and landings. After we were on the ground I hopped out of the ship and my bag fell out after me. I was on edge so much I almost jumped a foot. The only time my nerves quiet down is when I get that shot of whiskey after interrogation. You really get the full effect of it because everybody's stomach is empty . I 'd say we get about one meal a day when we fly.

One thing that consoles me is that I'm always ready for death. If I could just go on one mission where we wouldn't see ships going down and death everywhere. I haven't seen any like that yet although I expected to see lots of missions where there were no casualties.

In the papers you see, "Heavies bombed this place and that place," but nothing is said of what takes place on them. Of course I realize there's the military standpoint too.

The gas these planes use on one single raid would keep a family car running day and night for seventy one years.

Spleth Mission No. 9, Sept. 30, 1944 (Saturday) (905 J)
Target: Munster, Germany

Assembled as briefed. Had a good ship, 905 J. Flew #3 lead squadron, low box. Held good formation all the way. Light flak over target. Saw ship in lead box hit and go down. Carried incendiaries.

Briol, October 1, 1944.

I woke up about five o'clock this morning (Sunday) and was waiting for the C. Q. to come in and wake us up for a raid but he didn't come. Man! What a lovely surprise! I turned over and went back to sleep till nine o'clock. I went to Mass at eleven o'clock.

I got myself a piece of flak apron by hook and crook. I'm going to put a small stiffener in it. I have it under me in the Ball Turret and when the flak gets heavy, I pull it over the window. It would slow down a small piece of flak and keep shattering glass from hitting me in the eyes and face.

We got paid today, too. Base pay but no flying pay. I made another stripe. I'm Staff Sergeant now. It doesn't bring our buddies back, though.

Yesterday a ghost Fortress came back from Germany. It flew over England here and headed out to sea again towards Ireland. The crew was either all dead or there was no one in it.

I saw some articles in the British papers which said the English have destroyed just about all the Luftwaffe fighters. Man, oh man, what a laugh. We've seen more German fighters, havoc and destruction than any one person could think of. I don't think I've mentioned any real bloody details. I guess it's too unpleasant.

I never knew how soft, and I might as well say yellow, I could be, until I got over here. I know darn well, though, that there's no one that goes into combat, that isn't scared. It would be easier to die once but you die many times. These are my feelings now, but when everything is all over I'll probably look back and see how silly all this scribbling is. One thing about this air war, when a man gets "it" there's nothing left of him. No matter how much these Fortresses can take it, there are always losses in a fighter attack or flak barrage. When those FW -190's hit you with their cannon you drop like a clay pigeon.

Welch, October 1, 1944

Whenever we fly a mission, I look in the next day's Stars and Stripes to find out what targets it reports were hit the day before, along with an assessment of the damage done to the targets. The articles also report how many aircraft were lost by each side. I take all that with a grain or two of salt. But I underline the name of our target, and cut the article out and save it.

Briol, Monday October 2, Group Mission 130, Crew Abort

We had to abort today, in other words, we had to turn back before we hit enemy territory. While we were still over Belgium, our no. 2 engine started smoking and vibrating. Something hit us, I don't know what. It hit the plexiglass dome in the nose, breaking it and missing Ozzie and the Navigator. One of our gas tanks started leaking, so we thought. Something was gushing all over the wing in back of No. 2 engine. Instead of taking a chance of being blown up in a flak area, we turned back. We couldn't keep up, we were falling behind and losing altitude anyway. We feathered No. 2 prop. and came in on three engines with our full bomb load.

We were supposed to have bombed Kassel. It's a really rough target like the one we had the other day.

After crossing the channel we flew on over Dover. We could see the white cliffs of Dover rising out of the sea long before we got there. The British started shooting at us, too, as we passed over the coast. It wasn't high altitude flak. They just don't take any chances, because the Germans also have some of our Fortresses (captured).

There have been cases where Fortresses have joined our formations over enemy territory and no one thought anything of it. Their purpose was to come and see how high we were and radio our altitude to Germans on the ground who would get our range and we'd wonder why the flak was so accurate.

The Navigator of a crew in this hut was hit today. I'm sure even the "old timers" before us have never seen missions like some of these. It drives me almost crazy. I can't get the picture out of my mind of twenty enemy fighters coming at us abreast with their machine guns and cannons blazing and Fortresses blowing up around us and falling in flames and there we are almost alone as our fighters come in and help us out.

It makes me feel good anyway that my folks are provided for. They'd get $10,000 besides six months pay which would be flying pay and base pay for an extra stripe.

Spleth Mission No. 10A, October 2, 1944 (Monday)
Target: Kassel, Germany

Hard luck--everything O. K. till enemy territory was in sight. Glycol started to leak. Couldn't tell if it was glycol or gasoline--got a hole in astrodome about the same time from ship ahead. Decided not to trust luck too far and aborted. Feathered (#2) engine to prevent fire hazard.

Welch, October 2, 1944

I flew in the left seat for a mission to Kassel today. We got a fluid leak on the left wing on the way in and turned back because it looked like gasoline. We feathered No. 2. I got a short in my electrically heated shirt, and was getting burned; had to turn the thing off. With no heat from the cabin heat system (operated by No. 2 engine) I really got cold. Turned out the leak was glycol from the cabin heat system boiler. No mission credit.

Briol, Tuesday October 3, 1944

We flew a practice mission today, three boxes of twelve planes each. We flew at about 20,000 feet around the central part of England. Our tail gunner, (Harry) says, "I get cold and yellow chills up and down my spine before every mission." Goes for all of us.

Spleth, Mission No. 10B, Cologne, Germany Scrubbed.

Briol
Crew Mission No. 9, Group Mission No. 131, Thursday, Oct. 5

Our target for today was Cologne. We were to destroy the marshalling yards. I haven't time to say much about it. It wasn't very deep into Germany. Quite close to the lines. One bad thing about it, it's right in the Ruhr, (Happy Valley) where you get a solid wall of flak all the time. It was bad weather today. Ground wasn't visible, neither was the target. That's where our PFF ships (radar) come in handy. Another thing, the flak is not so accurate because they can't see us and when they use radar to track us, our chaff throws them off. No fighters attacked our group. The fighters usually show up in deep penetrations into Germany.

Got up at three o'clock this morning. Received, ate breakfast, briefed and then put the guts into the guns etc. It's getting cold around here and it's miserable putting your guns in, etc. At high altitude it was 43 degrees below zero. On the last few missions I've had my heated suit turned up all the way and I was still freezing. I'm getting more and more scared on each mission. As time goes on you find out things that can happen to you that you never dreamed of before.

It was supposed to be the Cologne marshalling yards, but the city caught blazes too. We had to go right over the Ruhr Valley. We battled intense flak for over an hour.

We almost started blazing away at some of our own fighters, for the simple reason that we can't even be sure they are our own fighters, because the Germans are using some of our captured P-51's in combat. Some of them pointed their noses toward us, and we were waiting for that flash of flame along the wings, which means they're blazing away at us.

We used a lot of chaff today which threw off the radar for the enemy antiaircraft guns. We used some evasive action but still came close to getting it. We were tossed around a little here and there. We were over six miles high for a while. I saw flak bursts creeping up from behind on the ship flying our right wing. I think it was hit kind of heavy because it fell out of formation and started straggling. Thank God we didn't have to watch anything really horrible today.

Our vapor trails were especially heavy, streaming out for miles and miles behind us. Germans can see you coming long before you hit enemy territory, and another thing, in those vapor trails enemy fighters can come up behind you and you may not be able to see them no matter how hard you strain your eyes. Some of the other groups were attacked by fighters but they let us alone today.

We were so tired today after the mission we could hardly take the guts out of our guns and load our equipment onto the truck. After we got our shot of whiskey we felt much better.

When we descended today my Ball Turret became coated with a sheet of ice. At high altitude you always have a big cake of ice down the front of your heated suit from your breath as it is exhaled through the oxygen mask. Every once in a while we have to squeeze our masks to break up the ice cakes in them in order to breathe.

There are a million things on these missions that can cause instant death. Today Ozzie's oxygen system failed and he had to use a "walk around" bottle. That made one man less to fight off the enemy if they attacked.

Today we carried twelve bombs, each weighing 500 lbs. We also had 2300 gallons of gas per ship to make the trip. We entered through Belgium and came out through Belgium. We can't drop any bombs west of the fighting lines in case our ship is falling behind, not even if we are straggling, because our troops are below.

Spleth, Mission No. 10C, Oct 5, 1944 (Thursday) (537)
Target: Cologne, Germany (Flew No. 6 in High Box)

After having scrubbed this the day before, we got up in the rain, but took off with blue sky above. Ran into haze and overcast at target. There was plenty of flak and contrails, but no fighters. Climbed above overcast on way back to above 29,000, almost 30,000! Let down after overcast broke up.

Battle damage consisted of a flak hole under tail gunner's seat. Landed O. K.

Briol
October 6, 1944, Crew Mission No. 10, Group Mission No. 132

We bombed Stargard today. It was in the Berlin area, so it was a very deep penetration. It was the other side of Berlin, practically on the border of Poland. It was a perilous trip, nearly all over the North Sea and Baltic Sea. We passed over Denmark and just south of Sweden (the airman's paradise), then south into Germany. We went back the same way.

It was a long, long tense trip. On the way over we had to go through a flak barrage as we passed over a bunch of German ships in a harbor. There was a bunch of German seaplanes down there too.

On the way back we dropped kind of low and watched our fighters give those boats and seaplanes the works. They strafed heck out of them. From the looks of things they killed everyone in those boats. We watched the bullets splattering in the water and the seaplanes burning. Most of the ships were blowing up and burning.

There were enemy fighters in the target area, but they didn't do much damage today. Quite a bit of flak to keep us sweating it out. On the last bomb in the rack I still write with chalk, "TO ADOLPH, FROM MARCELLA". On our way back, when we had passed over the North Sea again, we could relax. I left my turret, it wasn't so cold then, we had dropped down to about 5,000 feet. I was so tired, I fell asleep in the waist in a couple of minutes.

Spleth Mission No. 11, Oct 6, 1944, (Friday) (Flew No. 6 in Lead box, in ship No. 051 from the 749th Squadron).
Target: Primary, Politz, Germany: Secondary, Stargard, both near Stettin.

This was a long haul. We assembled briefed + 2. Saw a little flak as we crossed the Jutland Peninsula, but not close. Went in for a very smooth bomb run. Bombed secondary. No flak, no fighters. Came back in loose formation, had plenty of gas; landed with about 100 gallons in each tank.

Welch, October 6, 1944. Primary, Politz, Secondary, Stargard, hit Secondary.

We couldn't see Politz today because it was covered with clouds. so we dropped our bombs on the airfield at Stargard.

We heard later that Stargard is a Luftwaffe training field, and our bombs fell in the middle of a graduation ceremony.

I've written Mom and Dad and told them not to be too sad if I don't come back from all this. I've had a good life with opportunities and interesting challenges I could never have had in any other country in the world. And I'm very glad to have grown up in such a good family and with such good friends. Flying is what I like to do, and my contribution to a better world for all of us.

CHAPTER V

THE GOING GETS ROUGHER

Briol
Saturday, October 7, 1944, Crew Mission No. 11,
Group mission 133

We bombed Politz today, on the other side of Berlin, in the same area we bombed yesterday. All I can say is, a man can stand only so much. There were enemy fighters in the area, too. We took the same route we took yesterday. The same terrifying route. We had very heavy losses. It was a maximum effort. We lost three more men out of this hut. There are only three crews in here so it's quite a blow.

All three ships in the lead element were shot down over the target. We were right behind them. We were hit over fifty times, holes everywhere. Our ship quivered and shook until I thought it would fall apart. Every direction I looked flak was bursting. I must have prayed out loud. I could even smell the flak through my oxygen mask.

Colonel Luper, our group commander was lost. He was leading the group over the target. He flew very seldom but he got it today. His ship was ahead of us and we saw his Fortress get a direct hit. It caught fire immediately. All four engines were blasted from the plane. It fell and started to break up like a toy plane. I think two men got out.

The ship flying on our left wing got a direct hit in the nose. It almost crashed into us out of control. One man's body was hanging halfway out of what was left of the nose, most of his clothes blasted off. Equipment and stuff were falling out of the holes in the ship. I don't know what happened then.

I was sweating even at 40 below. They really had our range, every time a shell burst our ship jumped and quivered. Our whole formation was broken up. The lead crew was gone, so we dropped our bombs, whether they hit the right place or not. In the ball I was practically looking the bursts in the face as they tracked us along and kept exploding right under me. I thought we'd never get out of it. I pulled my piece of flak suit over the ball window and hung my head over the sight and just prayed.

We pulled off to the left since we were all alone (formation busted up) and joined another formation as protection against fighters. I had my hand on the turret door handles ready to make a break for dear life. There was a hole in the nose where a piece of flak came through and missed Ozzie by one inch again.

We headed northwest out over the Baltic Sea, then back over Denmark. Halfway over the North Sea two of our tanks went dry and I was afraid we'd have to land in the North Sea. We had to leave the formation and headed for the English coast alone. Our gas was almost gone. We had ten minutes gas left when we sighted the field. We gave the distress signal with flares and we came in ahead of other ships.

Back in the states they think we're having an easy time of it. 4 F's healthier and stronger than I am are living a life of ease. I shouldn't kick though, I have a lot to fight for. Sometimes, though, I feel as if I can never face another mission. I feel like refusing to fly sometimes, whether they throw me in the guardhouse, court martial me or anything. Something keeps me going.

Spleth Mission No. 12, October 7, 1944
Target: Politz, Germany

Also near Stettin. Assembled as briefed. Had a hard time keeping up during climb, pulled 2400 rpm and 38-40". Crossed the Jutland Peninsula O. K. No fighters.

Went into bomb run and hit the world's worst flak. It's the worst I ever saw. I got into position O. K. for the run, but the leader went down with the Colonel. Jennings salvoed and left (#3), also the deputy took out. I had started to follow the deputy to the right, so I continued to the right, on out over the H_2O. Got back into formation already low on gas. Flew very loose formation after crossing over the Peninsula (we received more flak there). Came on in sweating out gas, 1600 (rpm) and about 26-28". Landed with practically no gas.

Had a flak hit in the nose--had to change right wing panel, two Tokyos and #2 main tanks. Had hits by #2 and #3 engines.

A real tough mission was Politz, Germany. And I do mean it was a BAD one. It was our eleventh mission, and I will never be able to forget it.

The target was the largest synthetic oil plant in Germany. By the way the flak came up we knew it was the largest.

The trip to the target was very uneventful. But all hell broke loose when we started down the bomb run. We had intense and accurate flak. They were coming so close that we could feel the concussion from them when they went off. In fact we were close enough to one of them that busted between our No. 2 engine and the nose, that it broke all the glass without a piece of flak coming through the plane.

It is hard to tell just what it was like to be up there. I haven't the words for it. Anyway, no one would believe me. That is unless he was up there. too.

One shell cut loose just in front of our nose. One large piece came through the nose at me and knocked me over. My flak suit stopped it. Later we found five others that came through at the same time. About 2/3 of the plexiglass came out of the nose. There was a lot of glass flying around and I got it in both eyes. I was completely blinded by it. (From then on, I wear my glasses; at that time I was one of those smart guys that didn't wear the Army equipment.) The shell hit just at bombs away. I was knocked back and couldn't drop ours. Braffman had to crawl over me and hit the bomb switch. The bombs dropped OK, but the doors wouldn't come up. Haynes had to go out into the bomb bay without a parachute and crank them up by hand. It was bad for him with all the flak flying around, but he got the job done. A few pieces of flak came through the bomb bay doors as he was cranking them up.

After we had dropped our bombs, we were thinking of getting out of there. I heard Spleth say,

"Where the hell is everyone?"

All the planes that were in front of us were gone. And we couldn't see anyone to the rear. Once again we were left all alone.

I got the sight of one eye back and saw the flak was hitting out in front of us again, and that they were beginning to track us. It was coming in at us in a straight line. That meant

Figure 11. B-17 Bomb Bay doors; electrically operated or hand cranked open and closed, or emergency released to open. (John F. Welch)

Reich Hit By 5,000 Bombers

Oct 7 H II   537

Germany underwent its greatest aerial assault of the war Saturday when more than 5,000 Allied bombers, mostly Fortresses and Liberators of the U.S. Strategic Air Forces, and fighters struck from Britain, France and Italy at key industrial and communications points from east to west and north to south.

The combined strength of more than 1,400 British-based bombers and upwards of 800 Italy-based B17s and B24s comprised the largest U.S. bomber force ever dispatched on a single operation.

Third Day in Row

This was the third successive day of large-scale operations by the Eighth Air Force and the biggest attacking force since June 20 when over 1,500 Eighth heavies went out.

The Eighth's losses were 51 bombers and 15 fighters against the destruction of 49 enemy craft in the air and on the ground, including four jet-propelled Nazi fighters.

Two Me262s were shot down by 1/Lt. Urban L. Drew, P51 pilot from Detroit, who became the first Eighth Fighter Command pilot to score a double kill over the Nazis' new type of interceptor in one day.

Maj. Richard E. Conner, P47 pilot from Vicksburg, Miss., also bagged an Me262, while three P51 pilots—1/Lts. Elmer A. Taylor, of Green Forest, Ark., Everett N. Farrell, of Superior, Ariz., and 2/Lt. Willard G. Erkamp, of Eagle Rock, Cal.—shared in destroying an Me163 jet-propelled fighter.

Oct 7 ★ II Oil Plants Hit

Escorted by more than 900 Thunderbolts, Mustangs and Lightnings of the Eighth and Ninth Air Forces, the Eighth heavies ranged over central, eastern and northeastern Germany, hammering synthetic oil plants at Politz, near the Baltic Sea; Ruhland, Magdeburg, Bohlen, Merseburg and Lutzkendorf. The latter three are in the Leipzig area, and Ruhland is northeast of Dresden.

Other targets included a Krupp tank works at Magdeburg; tank plants, aero-engine plant and locomotive works at Kassel; a chemical and explosive works at Clausthal-Zellerfeld, south of Brunswick; a Focke-Wulf 190 repair depot, airdrome and a motor transport plant at Zwickau, south of Leipzig, and an airfield at Nordhausen.

15th Strikes from South

Striking simultaneously from the south, the 15th Air Force heavies, shepherded by nearly 400 fighters, pounded two oil refineries and an oil storage depot in the Vienna area.

Meantime, over 800 Lancasters and Halifaxes of the RAF Bomber Command, with fighter escort, smashed at the Nazi reinforcement centers of Emmerich and Kleve in western Germany, while other Lancasters carried out a low-level attack on the dykes guarding Walcheren Island.

Ninth Supports Armies

More than 300 Marauders and Havocs of the Ninth Air Force Saturday plastered bridges and supply points servicing enemy troops battling the U.S. First and Third Armies.

Ninth fighter-bombers in great strength ranged through the Rhine Valley and behind the German armies from Saarbrucken to Dusseldorf, bombing and strafing airfields, canals laden with supply barges railroads and numerous artillery positions. About 200 enemy fighters were encountered.

Bad weather curtailed activity yesterday by British-based U.S. heavies.

Figure 12. News report, bombing of Politz (and other targets) on October 7, 1944. (U.S. Army *Stars and Stripes*)

they were really looking down the barrels at us. I called to Spleth over the interphone and said to turn her to the right. He not only took her to the right, but he put the old plane down in a dive. In a few seconds we were out of range of the flak in the back.

We lost a lot of planes on that raid, including the C. O. We were flying right behind him, and I saw his plane blow up not more than fifty feet in front.

On the way back we joined up with another squadron and started back with them. Our navigator said they were headed straight for another flak installation. It was a small island. We had had enough flak to suit us, so we left them. Sure enough they had flak shoot up at them. We were clear of it.

When we got back we started counting holes in the plane. Both wings were full of them. Holes were in all but two of the gas tanks. The waist was full of them, and the tail also had them. There were ten in the nose. One came within a few inches of Braffman, right across the navigation table. There were 50 to 75 holes altogether

Welch Mission No. 11, Group No. 133, Politz, October 7

Col. Luper led the mission, and several of the Group staff, including the Group Surgeon, were flying with him. Our position, as usual, was leading the low element, in the slot, just below the Group Lead aircraft, an airplane length or two behind him. It was a clear day, and unlike yesterday, the synthetic oil plant area of Politz was visible except for smoke screen. As we turned over the I. P., the high element and the left element moved out into their level positions just behind Lead. We continued in our slot position, so that the box formed a diamond, each corner an element of three ships.

About half way down the bomb run, we began picking up some flak, then all hell broke loose. The biggest, blackest bursts I have ever seen were ahead and to the sides of us. Every burst sounded like someone had hit the side of the airplane with a huge sledge hammer. The fire was deadly accurate, concentrating on the lead airplane. The flak gunners must have been sighting visually with 155 millimeter guns. Chaff was completely useless.

Suddenly, Luper's airplane was leaking oil and gasoline out of the wings, and No. 3 engine was on fire. I heard him say on the radio,

"Get that goddam formation in here!"

Then his airplane began a steep descent. We managed to avoid him, and looked for number two to drop our bombs on, while the carnage continued, but he was gone, too. Then we looked to the high element Lead, Angier, and dropped when he did.

Suddenly, there was no one in front of us, but we were out of the worst flak. We heard one of our ships, Jennings, call in, saying he was badly shot up, with wounded on board, and he was going to try to make it to Sweden. We finally joined up with some other airplanes. Everyone checked in on the interphone. Miraculously everybody was pretty much O. K. and all four engines were running. Angier picked up the lead.

When we headed over a known flak position, Braffmann warned us, so we turned away from the formation; we'd had enough flak for the day. Sure enough the rest of the formation got shot at some more.

We coasted in over England very low on gas, but finally landed safely. Once more our prayers had been answered.

Haynes earned his pay today. He not only cranked the bomb bay doors closed--coming in, we had him pumping a few gallons at a time among the tanks, to keep the engines running until we could get it on the ground

Briol
Sunday, October 5, 1944
.

Thank God we don't have to fly today. I don't think I could have taken it after what happened yesterday. I miss Legassa, Petty and Stowitz. They were in this hut quite a while. Part of their crew is still in here because they didn't fly yesterday.

It's miraculous how we made it yesterday. I don't see how our ship took the terrific barrage. It was quivering and shaking and sliding all over the sky. Someone was sure taking care of us and I'm grateful.

Our waist gunner (Byknish) is in a bad way. We all are but I don't think he'll be able to take another mission. Last night when he went to bed he was shivering and shaking. I don't blame him, it's a horrible business.

There were three ships at this base that were still in flying shape and they were actually going to make our crew fly one of them, what a blow! I was sweating it out all night but oh boy, the weather was really bad today.

It (the mission) was really bad today, too. Polebrook, a field next to us, sent up about fifteen planes and 2 came back.

It's been hell in the air since we've started these deep penetration missions. As the Germans are pushed back their fighters and guns are moved back and become more concentrated and we get the worst of it.

Back home, they think the war is won. There's a baseball game on the radio and one player throws his bat down. He's irritated because the game doesn't go the way he wants it to. Man, he's got lots of troubles. I probably sound bitter. Well, I guess I am, a little.

Flannery's crew was the one that was lost from this hut yesterday. Jennings and his crew (from some other hut) were not shot down but were hit quite badly. I think they made it to Sweden.

I had no idea we were going to have such a tough time of things. I hope we plastered some of those flak gun crews and positions yesterday. After we got over the target yesterday, when we looked back, I wondered how the dickens we ever made it. It was a horrible sight. The air was full of flak, fire and smoke as the other group came over the target. Our Fortresses were being plucked right out of the sky. I couldn't watch it. I could imagine the Germans below gleefully watching our men die. I also know that lots of Germans died below, too.

All our crew goes to church now. I just came back from 11 o'clock Mass. There was a happy surprise waiting for us when we came back. We finally got a 48 hour pass. Two more days to live for certain. We really need that rest. I think I'll go to London again. We were waiting a long time for that pass. They kept putting it off because there weren't enough crews, so we were overworked.

Briol
October 10, 1944

Came back from London about four o'clock today. Most

of our crew was there. Some of us slept in the Red Cross Hotel there.

Two robot bombs exploded nearby again while we were there. They both came about 11 o'clock at night. They seem to come about the same time each night. The first night the alert sounded and about five minutes later I heard that motor cycle sound coming closer, then it cut off and a few seconds later the tremendous explosion.

We visited a few more places in London, but not to a great extent. We rested mostly. Went to a couple of dances at the Red Cross at Picadilly Circus. Drank some English beer and got a little tipsy.

I went to a movie, "An American Romance". It made me pretty homesick.

We almost went up to Edinburgh, Scotland, on our 48 but decided it was a little too far.

We've got our little hut really fixed up here. (Time out to go out and get paid. I just got my flying pay for last month. Money doesn't mean anything to me now. All I want to do is keep my skin whole.)

As I was saying we have our walls lined with maps of every territory and the places marked where we have blasted. On our door we used to have our crew commanders' names, of Zeiler, Flannery and Spleth. It's just Spleth and Zeiler now.

Also on the door we have " Stop! Check your guns at the door!", and "Stop! Is this trip really necessary?" (That's for the C. Q. who comes to wake us up early in the morning.) Also, there's "Through these portals pass the world's tiredest mortals".

The name of our hut is "Sack Time Hovel". We have a cat in here to catch the rats and mice. You can see our bikes laying around almost any place outside the hut. I don't know what happened to the bikes that belonged to Flannery's crew who were shot down. The vultures around here probably got them. A lot of the guys took over their clothes and stuff but I just haven't the heart to do that sort of thing.

When I was in London I tried again to get something for the folks and Marcella for Christmas but I just can't seem to find anything. They haven't got anything. I was at Selfridge's in London and for such a big place they haven't much. Need coupons too. Poor imitations for Christmas cards.

Aachen is surrounded. We may be in destroying the city

if the Germans don't surrender. We're standing by.

Welch, 10 October 1944

Spleth and I agreed that London is not the place to go on pass, so we went to Edinburgh instead. We especially enjoyed a walking tour, which included Edinburgh Castle. The tour guide was an elderly Scot who told an almost continuous series of funny stories about the English. I've heard of the Scotch burr. He did talk differently.

He's not the only one. In our compartment on the train on the way back from Edinburgh were half a dozen British sailors from York. All we could understand of their conversation were the "four letter words" and the cuss words.

At least it was a relief to get away from the pressures of combat flying for a couple of days.

Briol
October 11, 1944.

Practice mission today. Weather is probably bad over Germany. Besides, we got in five new crews to replace those lost last time. They're so eager to get in their first mission. If they only knew what is in store for them.

I found out today that my claims for shooting down those fighters were recognized.

The practice mission was called off today because of bad weather. That gives us time to go to Mass and Novena this afternoon. It's raining and blowing right now and if it keeps up we won't fly tomorrow.

It's funny but we all feel secure when it rains. I love rain now. I realize we should be flying and getting the job over but I'm weak. It's hard to face death even though you know it's not helping the war any when you're not flying. I'll have time to write some letters now. I'll send my Air Medal home, too. I'll have time to wrap it up. I must get a great kick out of talking to myself like this.

I listen to the news now and then. I like to hear of our advances although we know the more they advance the harder it is on the airmen. It means deeper penetrations for us, more concentrated fighter and flak barrages for us. I'm afraid we'll

76

be up for lead crew, soon. I hope not. Look what has happened to all our lead crews. Look at what prizes the Germans have bagged these last few days.

I read in the paper today of a raid that took place a year ago over Munster in which a few bombers fought off hundreds of enemy fighters. It reminded me of our raid over Magdeburg not so long ago. It was a hell in the air if there ever was one. I know what those fellows went through on that raid of a year ago. I'm not proud to say though.

These missions are doing something to me that never can be corrected, I guess. It's the same with all the guys more or less.

Briol
October 13, 1944

Our target for today was to be Cologne but we didn't get to the target. The mission was scrubbed. I think it was called off because of weather over Germany. Cologne is really getting it. The entire 8th Air Force was to bomb it today. Our route today was to be the same as before. We got up early this morning and did a lot of work before take off. It was cold, too. I'm still glad it was scrubbed.

An alert sounded before and a robot bomb exploded nearby, it was the first bomb to ever come close to this base since I've been here.

We got in five more crews (new) these last two days. They're not operational yet but will be soon. They're sweating out their first mission yet. I wish they'd never have to fly that first mission or any of them for that matter. They haven't had their Baptism of flak and fighters yet.

Another reason I'm glad we didn't fly today is that Ozzie, our nose gunner, was sick and grounded. That meant we'd have to have a spare gunner take his place. Whenever the crew is busted up like that, it seems to destroy confidence and it seems like something always goes wrong. Our crew is just like a family. The other crew left in this hut is beginning to be like a family to us now, too. Harry our tail gunner says, "I'd just as soon trade places with the K.P.'s in the mess hall, then I could sit and watch these combat crew members come in with the worried looks on their faces."

Briol
Crew Mission No. 12, Group Mission No. 134, Saturday, Oct. 14

We bombed Cologne again today, the whole Eighth Air Force. Ran into bandits but we came out okay. There were ships lost but I don't think there were any lost from our box of twelve. Our lead ship had part of its nose blown off but I don't think anyone was injured seriously. There was a long barrage of flak but the Germans couldn't see where we were today, so they got few hits. We had one hole in a wing tank (gas) that I could almost stick my head through. The gas didn't leak out till we landed, though. One of those freaks.

We had one more hole near the nose but it wasn't bad. The one that hit in the wing wasn't far from my position. If it had hit my turret it would have blasted it to blazes. Our escort fighters were all over the place. They had quite a battle.

Today we carried fifteen 500 lb. bombs and three incendiary clusters, 2,400 gallons gas load. The flak was intense but it was inaccurate. They couldn't get our range.

Spleth Mission No. 13, Oct. 14, 1944 (Saturday)
No. 3, high flight, high box (954 Q)
Target: Cologne, Germany

Mission was scrubbed twice before. We finally made it today. Assembled as briefed + 6. Went in to target without much trouble. Not much battle damage. Hole in #3 gas tank and a few others. Have piece of flak that hit tank. No doubt they will say #13 is pretty easy.

Flak inaccurate, no fighters--cranked up bomb bays (doors) after bombs away.

Welch, Mission No. 12

After take off on each mission, Cornell flashes the Aldis lamp out the tail at regular intervals in the clouds to keep the following aircraft from chewing our tail off. Once on top the clouds we have to look for our formation lead, which fires colored flares to identify itself, red-green-red, for instance.

Once in position, we circle until we're formed up, and at the scheduled time the formation heads for the coast out point.

My early rising catches up with me about then, and while Spleth is flying the airplane, I have been known to go to sleep.

Briol
Sunday October 15, 1944 (Crew Mission No. 13) (Group Mission No. 135)

Today, (Sunday) we were on our way to Germany to bomb Cologne long before it was light. We were awakened about one o'clock this morning. Our route after we crossed the Channel was over Belgium up into Holland and down into Germany.

As we hit the fighting lines flak started coming up at us as usual and continued all through the Ruhr Valley. I don't know how many ships we lost. We turned at the I. P. onto the bomb run, dropping chaff to mess up the Germans' radar.

A piece of the flak shot through the bomb bay knocking out the system and the bomb bay doors would not open. Haynes got his crank and started in but they still wouldn't open. I had my guns ready for fighters and sweating out the flak and bomb bay doors at the same time.

All of a sudden, "wham" and most of our No. 4 engine was shot away. Fire, smoke and oil were pouring out of it. Another piece of flak went through the bomb bay, one through the waist knocking out the interphone and a lot of the electrical wiring. It hit one of the ammunition boxes for the waist guns, setting off some of the incendiary bullets but they didn't cause any damage. One went through the nose. One hit the window in the cockpit shattering it and one went through the tail grazing Harry's boot. The concussion almost knocked us silly.

We were almost over the target. Haynes pulled the emergency release for the bomb bay doors and they opened. Then our bomb releases wouldn't work and we salvoed them finally after we were past the target. We really blasted the city wide open, though. It was blotted from view by the pillars of smoke.

Our waist gunner was hollering, "Let's get out of here." but you couldn't hear him. We were flying on three engines now and falling back behind and losing altitude. We were left behind straggling. There wasn't enough left of the blasted engine to feather it. We would have been duck soup for enemy fighters, but there were some formations behind us and their escort fighters kind of looked after us.

Our bomb bay doors wouldn't close and Haynes was still standing there with his crank, hampered by his mask, flak suit, heated suit, intense cold and everything else. In the excitement he lost his flak helmet out the bomb bay and it went sailing down to Adolph below.

Everything was shot in the bomb bay, so we had to let the doors hang open and they held us back. Our engine, what was left of it, was only smoking now. We were doing only 130 miles an hour then, so it took us a long time cross Belgium, the Channel and then back to our base, but we made it.

We were all set to bail out a couple times. We hit some more flak before we got to friendly territory. I kind of figured we'd lose the rest of the engine when we landed. I was watching it. We no sooner hit the runway and that 1,000 lbs. of metal engine went crashing on the runway, but our skins are still whole.

The blasted ground crew had our lockers all locked up already. They figured we were shot down and had the rest of our equipment all confiscated. Then they looked at us, as much as to say, "Oh you're back, I suppose you left lots of work on the ship for us to do." They worry about their stripes, we worry about our lives. They can have my stripes and wings. All I want is my skin whole.

Yesterday a ground equipment man gave me the dickens for opening the extra equipment bag we always take along. He wanted to know why I broke the safety. I'm always responsible for the bag in our ship. I told him I always lay aside the extra chute and one of our crew needed a mask. He said that bag is for emergency only.

I got sore. I told him,

"Listen buddy, you never know when there's going to be an emergency." I also told him something I won't mention.

If there's anything a man hates it's to come back from a tough all day mission tired and jittery, nerves almost shot and be kicked around by a ground crew man who doesn't know what combat is like. After a mission someone is liable to find a couple gun barrels wrapped around his neck if he crosses us up.

I guess this is the wrong attitude, but a guy can't help it after doing this for a while. After receiving Viaticum this morning, Father Ludder told us we'd be back for 5:30 Mass this afternoon. We made it back all right and we got to Mass. A priest always came over from another base but now we have one here permanently.

I hope we get a little sleep tomorrow instead of flying. About the only time we don't fly is when we lose or damage a lot of ships or the weather is real bad.

One of my buddies from Langley Field got it today. He flies the ball (or rather flew) like I do. A piece of flak came right through the metal door in the ball right into his back.

When I go home (if), I want to forget all this and have just the very simplest things in life. I've just realized how much more I could have done for my Mother and Dad to make life easier for them. I'll do everything for Marcella that I can possibly do.

Spleth Mission No. 14, October 15, 1944 (Sunday) (101 F)
Target: Cologne, Germany

Tail end Charley, lead box.

A little rough today. Everything S. O. P. Night takeoff. Messed up everything at I. P. A lot of flak. Couldn't get bomb bay doors open at first. Finally got them open. Haynes salvoed bombs from bomb bays by pulling knob. # 4 engine got hit, lost oil before we could feather it. Couldn't get bomb bays closed. #3 amplifier went out. Lost formation at target. #4 prop ran away till it (the engine) froze. Lot of vibration till front of engine broke loose allowing prop to windmill. All communications were shot out except interphone from radio room forward. Tried to shake prop over channel by diving, but no good. Came in to land by flares on (runway) 24, bomb bays open.

Lost prop at intersection of 24 and 16.

Ammunition can in waist hit. Window by me hit. Holes everywhere. Glad to get back. Came back from target alone except for good P-51 support. No enemy fighters.

Ozenberger, Mission No. 13, October 14, 1944

Our thirteenth mission on October 15 was to Cologne. We hit the marshalling yards, not far from the great Cathedral.

It was our second mission there in a row. The flak was heavy, and we got a direct hit on our No. 4 engine. It caught fire, but was put out by diving the ship.

We got a lot of other holes, but don't remember how many. No. 4 was vibrating so much it shook the whole plane. The prop was running away and couldn't be controlled. It looked as if it would fall off at any time. But it didn't.

When we got over the Channel, Spleth dived the plane to try and drop the prop off. But it wouldn't fall. So we brought it back to the base and landed. As soon as we hit the ground, the prop dropped off, bounced up and ripped a large hole in the wing. It was really something to see. All members of the crew were safe.

Briol, Monday October 16, 1944

We didn't fly today. It was raining cats and dogs this morning. Lovely rain! We just lay in our bunks this morning. The First Sergeant came in and said they were going to have an inspection at 11 o'clock. We just opened our eyes and looked at him, "To heck with you Sergeant," and rolled over and went back to sleep. To blazes with getting up after getting up on these cold midnights and throwing our lives away over Germany. Our cat caught some mice last night. A week ago someone stole Harry's (our tail gunner) bike. The other night someone stole mine. Paid five pounds for it too. No doubt it's some of the ground crew. A lot of that sort of thing goes on around here. You're liable to lose anything you own, unless you keep an eye on it.

Welch, October 16, 1944

A special duty for crew officers is censoring V-Mail and regular letters written by enlisted crew members (not our own); no military secrets permitted. Byknish and Grybos write home in Polish, so their letters go to London to be censored. I did not mark out a comment by a newly arrived gunner to his wife: "I damn near got laid in Grand Island."

Some crew members have codes to let wives know when they've flown missions and how many.

Briol
Tuesday, October 17, 1944, Crew Mission No. 14,
Group Mission No. 136

We gave it to Cologne again today. We're really giving them the works. Of course, we suffer great losses doing it, too, that no one will ever hear about. There were a lot of fighters in the vicinity today. The flak in the Ruhr Valley was terrifying as usual. On the bomb run after we had the bomb bay doors open, the flak was really pounding away. There were about eight planes left in our box out of twelve.

There were a bunch of tremendous blasts right next to our ship. Our plane was jumping and skipping like a jack rabbit. The plane on our right took the worst of it, and one right above us. I saw a flash of flame in no. 4 engine on the ship to our right. It fell out of formation right away. So did the one above us. I don't know what happened to the one above us or the other two who were lost.

As our bombs were away and we were leaving the target, I saw one plane get it in the box behind us. One man was blown through the fuselage. There was a big puff of smoke and then it fell out flaming. After about the third turn it exploded to bits. I think it was the only plane that fell out of the box behind us.

I didn't see where our bombs hit today. The target was covered by clouds right after bombs away. We had two holes in our nose. There was one through our left Tokyo tank, big enough to stick your head through. We transferred fuel to another tank before it leaked out. We had one hole through the radio room, and one through the waist. We didn't know it then, but one flak burst blew out a tire.

The bursts didn't have a "whump" sound today but they had a "krump" sound like the devil beating on the side of our plane with his coal shovel.

I was up in the nose for the landing; as our wheels touched there was a heck of a vibration as our right tire hit without any air in it. I was watching it and in a few seconds it was ground to spaghetti and we were running on the rim. It pulled us off the runway on to the soft ground. The wheel dug into the ground until the right wing tip almost touched.

We've ruined more ships so far. The one we brought back last time won't fly for a long time and neither will this one.

It seems like we always get shot up on every mission but we get back. Just so we don't get it like I've seen so many get it, "all at once" and nothing left of the planes and crews except a tremendous explosion.

After the mission today I got two shots instead of the usual one. It made me pretty happy. Spleth told me it was the first time he saw me laugh in a long time. I don't feel any too good tonight. Got some kind of chills or something. I caught cold after high altitude on the last mission. Had trouble with my ears blocking up at high altitude today. We walked back to the hut in the rain tonight.

I've got to fly every time the crew does though. I saw what happened to the two guys who are left from the other crew that went down because they didn't fly with them. Their spirit is broken. They're up for a flak leave.

It's strange how proud, beautiful and tight our formations are when they leave the English coast east for Germany. When we come back we look like a whipped dog. All spread out, straggling, props feathered, engines smoking and some just not there.

Spleth Mission No. 15, October 17, 1944 (Tuesday)
No. 4, low section, low box (954 Q)
Target: Cologne, Germany

Another night takeoff, pretty dark assembly. Box went in to target by itself. Good run PFF, but in flak quite some time. Dropped bombs O. K. and came back in formation. Landed with flat, but did not know it till landed. Right tire. Ran off runway to right side, no damage to plane.

Battle damage, big hole in left wing.

Briol, Wednesday, October 18, 1944

We were all ready to take off for Kassel and bomb it but it was scrubbed before we took off. I was sure glad about it. We would have had to fight it out with over 200 enemy fighters. That was the expected opposition. On one of the last raids to Kassel, 28 out of 38 B-24 Liberators were lost.

Our crew has its own little song. It goes like this; "Oh scrub, scrub, scrub this mission, I don't want to fly; Oh scrub,

scrub, scrub this mission, I don't want to die."

When we leave the European theater we'll be searched for accounts of missions such as this, so I'll have to smuggle it out some way.

Poor John Byknish, our waist gunner, is in an awful bad way. He's completely broken down. His nerves are shot. He won't be able to fly again. I know partly how he feels. I'm going to stick it out though.

We're all under a terrible strain. It's impossible to describe what something like this does to a man. It's hard to transfer feelings from one person to another. I guess no one will ever know what a life this is, unless he goes through it. I expected this, but it's entirely different when you're actually in it.

Welch, Wednesday, October 18, 1944

The Flight Surgeon asked Spleth and me to stop in and visit with him this afternoon. He told us he is grounding Byknish because he can't take these missions any more. It's no mark against John, he says he wants to fly, but the Doc says every man has a breaking point, and John has reached it. Actually he went to see the doctor only because the other gunners urged him to. They say he's been calling out fighters and flak when there aren't any, and they're very worried about him.

From now on, we'll fly with a spare gunner in the waist, probably a former member of a crew that has been lost on an earlier mission. A replacement will eventually be assigned.

There are three theories about surviving a tour. One says that the odds are so against it that each time one flies a mission, his chances are that much worse. The second theory says that each time you survive, your chances are improved that much. The third theory says that one's odds are the same for each mission, neither improving nor worsening. My tendency is to accept whatever odds there are, and to hope for somehow getting out of this with a whole skin.

Briol, Thursday, October 19, 1944, Crew Mission No. 15
Group Mission No. 137

Mannheim was the target we bombed today. It's in the

southeastern part of Germany in the Frankfurt area. I've only got a few minutes to write before I get a few winks. We landed a short time ago.

Today our group was the only one to hit this target. It was the longest bomb run to the target we ever had. Those bomb bay doors were open for ages before we got the bombs away. The lead ship was lost for a while and we were floundering all over, before we got the target. It was cloudy all over Germany it seemed.

The flak was terrifying and for a change we had only one hole in our ship but it was a big one. We had a heavy hit in the tail section, which bounced us around plenty. Besides black explosions we had a new type of flak barrage blasted at us today. It was different colored explosions. I don't know much about it. I didn't see any ships fall out of our box today. I didn't watch any of the other boxes. One ship was hit pretty bad and it straggled.

A lot of men are in the hospital from today's mission from being frozen at high altitude. One tail gunner lost his life in our box from lack of oxygen because his hose became unplugged. We always report every so often on our oxygen from our position but it only takes a few seconds.

In a break in the clouds I could see the flak guns on the ground below blasting away at us. It looked as if there were a thousand.

I couldn't help taking notice of the clouds today even while my life was at stake. They looked like huge billowy mountains rising out of nothing but there was death under them, on top and all over them.

We had another man fly the waist today for John Byknish. John is in the hospital. We used to call him "Big John". He was the biggest and huskiest man on the crew. We're all scared but it got him first. I think it was the Magdeburg raid that finished him off. Toward the last he'd go crazy with fear when we'd get into enemy territory. He couldn't sleep at night. His thoughts were driving him crazy. He surely did his best, too. On the last raid he made with us, we saw a flaming Fortress falling and I know John saw it too. That's the last time he flew.

In some of the hospitals there are a lot of pitiful cases of "flak happy men". I'm probably a little flak happy myself. I hope they lower the number of missions.

86

If I didn't have someone waiting for me back home I'd go stark raving mad. I believe I'm going to come out of this hell all right. When a man lets his thoughts run away with him and he starts believing every mission is going to be his last, he's finished, that's all there is to it. If I don't come back, it will be God's will.

It was over 60 degrees below zero Centigrade at high altitude today. I thought it used to get cold in Minnesota. Without a heated suit we'd be frozen stiff. If any part of our body would be exposed to that slip stream we'd lose it.

Blazes, just ready to get into bed and we find out we have to fly for a couple hours tonight to slow time a ship.

Spleth Mission No. 16, October 19, 1944 (Thursday)
No. 4, low section, low squadron (899 S)
Target: Mannheim, Germany

What a mess! Time was held up 2 hours--took off at 10 instead of 8. Assembled at briefed + 1.

Ran into clouds at target. Kept in formation, climbing on bomb run. Small flak on bomb run. Saw some red bursts. No flak at bombs away. Formation scattered all over sky. Finally got into formation, came back out. Left formation at English coast and brought camera in.

Called Zeiler on VHF for smoking engine on return.

Slight battle damage in tail.

Briol, Friday, October 20

No flying today but a lot of lectures and discussions. I got the whole story on the death of one of our tail gunners from lack of oxygen on yesterday's raid. We were flying at over 30,000 feet. Temperature up there was about 60 degrees below. One of the ships was straggling and the crew commander told the crew to assemble in the radio room to balance the ship to get more speed. They all left their positions and came up. The tail gunner came up without his drag around bottle holding his breath. When he went back he also went without his bottle. On the oxygen check he didn't answer. The waist gunner went back and saw him moving and thought he was okay and reported it. He didn't answer on the next check so the ball gunner went back with his bottle and found him all purple. He turned on the emergency oxygen but it was too late. They found out this guy didn't have much training in oxygen discipline. When I get in and out of my turret I usually hold my breath because I don't have far to go until another connection.

To top things off they have to give us the usual monotonous venereal disease lectures.

The contrails (vapor trails) were terrific yesterday. As long as they stream out behind you it's hard to see enemy fighters coming in on you.

We visited "Big John" in the hospital this afternoon. They have no nurses around here, some medics, etc. There are a few Limey Red Cross women. Some English women hang around to see how much they can take the guys for. They get chased out.

There was a dance at the Aero Club tonight. I went over in my fatigue clothes and watched it for a while. Got some coffee and doughnuts. Came back and now I'm going to bed.

Probably another rough day tomorrow. I always have that sick feeling in my stomach whenever I know we're going to fly. Someday I'll be able to go to bed and sleep in peace, knowing that I won't have to get up at midnight and go face death and see it. I hope we don't use fragmentation bombs again. It usually means we kill a lot of people.

I found out that the hole in our tail section on our last raid was made by a whole projectile passing through it. They're supposed to explode on impact but by the grace of God it didn't. If it would have, we'd all have been blown to bits.

Hot dog, the tail gunner from Zeiler's crew just came in from the orderly room and said there was a stand down for tomorrow which means we probably won't fly tomorrow. Of course, we have been disappointed that way before. I know I should want to fly and help the war along but I'm so blasted scared that I feel like shouting for joy when we're grounded. I hope our crew and Zeiler's can finish their or our missions together. We're the only crews left in this hut besides the two men from Flannery's crew who didn't fly with him the day he went down near Berlin. From what we saw none of them lived and if any got to the ground alive and were caught by civilians they were undoubtedly killed.

The civilians are very unfriendly, now. If we parachute

into Germany our only protection is our pistols. There's no underground in Germany to help a man like there used to be in France. You really can't blame them. We go over again and again destroying their cities, homes, families, etc. Although our main aim is to destroy military objectives there are so many bombs dropped that everything gets hit. All I can say, it's a horrible job and I hope it's finished soon.

Briol, Saturday, October 21

Lovely fog out today. No flying. We cleaned and adjusted the guns on ship 591. That was the ship that was originally assigned to us. We used it once and it has sat in sub depot ever since. We got it shot up in the Magdeburg raid. Some other crew used it some time after and got it shot up and crash landed it. It's being repaired but I hate to fly in it. Last two ships we brought back also went to sub depot.

We had a news lecture on other theaters of war. Also a lecture on the enemy jet fighters. In yesterday's raid on Cologne (we weren't on it) 36 enemy fighters showed up. Eleven of our fighters were shot down. About thirteen enemy fighters fell. They don't seem to say much about our losses but I've seen plenty of our fighters go down with my own eyes on other raids we made.

Ozzie and I are going to Peterborough tonight, so I'll have to shower and shave, in cold water, naturally.

Briol
Sunday, October 22, Crew Mission No. 16, Group Mission No.
138

Today, (Sunday) we hit Hannover, Germany, bombed heck out of it. I didn't actually see many casualties today, which gives me much more hope and courage. We bombed by PFF (radar) because there were many clouds below us. Since we were close to Berlin we expected about 200 enemy fighters. They didn't get through to us this time. Our escort fighters were on the ball. We saw plenty though.

I'm usually interrogated because I'm the Ball Turret man and I'm in a position to see things that no one else sees. I don't especially like it. I always see the dog fights, where the bombs hit, our own planes falling, and flak, when enemy fighters come in low, nobody can see them like I can. Today I wasn't afraid of the flak for a change. I watched it exploding everywhere but they couldn't get our range. We didn't have a single hole in our own ship.

Besides us throwing out chaff over the target, some escort fighters went over and threw out chaff before we got there. It really messed up their radar.

Our group was first over the target. Our ship was No. 3 in the high element in the high box. Before we got to the target our two wingmen fell behind and straggled, one with a feathered engine, so we were alone again and had to hug the rest of the box as protection against fighters. Our gas load was 2,500 gallons. Our bomb load was six 500 lb. bombs and six 500 lb. incendiary bombs. Our route was over the Channel, Holland and into Germany. It was the same out.

While we were up there battling it out with the Jerries the Military Police were down there battling it out with our bicycles. The rest of our crew lost their bikes to the M. P.'s because they weren't registered. I found out that's where mine went, too. Also Harry's. While I went into the Aero Club for doughnuts and coffee the M. P.'s came along and took my bike. We'll probably have to pay a fine to get them back. The brave M. P.'s, I'd love to have them beside me on a raid and see what they'd do.

Last night Ozzie and I went to Peterborough. We caught a G. I. truck in. We ate supper there and then went to an English movie, (English Without Tears).

It's surprising how many of these airmen don't even believe in God, so they say. They say it's luck. How could it be luck, like in our case, to have planes shot down all around us? Of course, we've been shot up again and again but we've always limped back. I don't think our Engineer/Top Turret gunner believed much at first but on one of our last raids he was praying out loud as I often do. I know because he accidentally pressed his mike switch and you could hear, "God take care of us." over the interphone.

Last night I was dreaming of Marcella, when all of a sudden I was awakened into a life of horror. The C. Q. was shaking me and saying, "Spleth's Crew? Breakfast at two thirty, briefing at three," and there I was with my thoughts of getting up early and going out to face the Germans. "What a blow!" I felt like putting my .45 to my head and pulling the trigger.

Spleth Mission No. 17, October 22, 1944 (Sunday)
No. 3 high element, high squadron (506 J)
Target: Hannover, Germany

Assembled as briefed + 2. Instrument takeoff. Lead of element dropped out. Took over lead, #2 man dropped out (Hollis). Very little flak at target. No hits. Bombs away at target. Plane O. K. Came back and landed O. K. Visibility very poor on landing. Easy mission. One of Gamboa's boys rode waist gunner.

Briol, Tuesday, October 23, 1944

No flying today although we were on the loading list. Our whole crew was sweating it out this morning. I woke up about one o'clock this morning from force of habit. It started getting light outside. We were watching it through a crack in the blackout curtain but still we weren't alerted. We're supposed to get a 48 hour pass tonight. I'm afraid it will be cancelled though. Ozzie and I were planning on going up to Scotland. We were going to sleep at the Red Cross in Peterborough and then pull out in the morning. Since I have time now, I'm going to write some letters. I wish it would be as convenient to write letters here as it was back in the States.

Welch, October 24, 1944

When the ground forces liberated the "Low Countries", they left some German flak batteries cut off along the coast, probably not considering the benefits of taking them worth the cost of going after them. Maybe the Allied Forces thought the isolated enemy units would see the hopelessness of the situation, and surrender.

Well, they're still there, and still have ammo. You'd think our mission planners and navigators would give them a wide berth, but they don't. There are two batteries in particular that like to fire at bomber formations. We call them Hans and Fritz. If you try to fly between them, you'll get holes from one or the other, or both.

At each mission briefing, we're shown the locations and estimated numbers of anti-aircraft guns in the flak batteries along our routes. They get moved around quite a bit, so our routing changes trying to avoid them. Along the Rhine River we have special problems. The German defenses have loaded anti-aircraft guns on barges (flak barges) and move them up and down the river according to their own schemes of things. They've been a special nuisance on our missions to Cologne.

CHAPTER VI

ARE THEY GETTING EASIER?

Briol
Thursday, October 26, 1944, Crew Mission No. 17
Group Mission No. 140

We bombed the German city of Bielefeld today. I feel pretty good tonight. We did a good job and I don't think our losses were very high.

The thing that really makes me feel good is the fact that a letter from Marcella was waiting for me when I got back. I never forget my little message to Adolph from her, on our bombs.

We led the whole Eighth Air Force over the target today. Although we bombed by radar there were breaks in the clouds and I could see huge fires and explosions. We bombed ordnance plants, so there was plenty to blow up, powder and ammunition exploding. Naturally we went through the flak barrages but they couldn't get our range. There were blood red explosions around us again today. I can't figure out that colored flak.

We usually use some waist gunner now, that's for spare purposes. These guys have usually lost part of their crew and fly with other crews who have lost men.

Our route today was over the Channel, Holland, the Zuider Zee and into Germany; same out. It's dangerous coming over the Zuider Zee. Coming back we usually start descending and it seems like they always blast some of our ships around that spot. We've been in contact with enemy fighters quite often but it has been nothing like some of the earlier missions we were on and especially not as bloody as the Magdeburg raid.

We got back quite late tonight because our takeoff time was delayed quite a bit this morning because of bad weather. There was bad weather when we returned, too. Runways were lit up so we could see them in the fog.

When we got back we had pretty good chow. We actually had ice cream, too. It tasted pretty good even if it was made of powdered milk. That's what we always get, powdered milk and eggs. When I go to town I always buy meals there. What a menu! Can't get much of anything. Usually costs about seven shillings.

Our radio gunner (Grybos) just tied a string to the cat's tail and he's standing there laughing. First time he laughed for a long time. That's what combat does to us. It's surprising how affectionate we are to animals, though.

Spleth Mission No. 18, October 26, 1944 (Thursday)
No. 1, low element   (537 V)
Target: Bielefeld, Germany

Very easy mission. Assembled as briefed.

Instrument takeoff. Went through some clouds on climb and almost stalled out.

I did not see any flak over the target. Some claim there was some very low.

Came back in formation, made separate let down through clouds. Visibility very poor again.

One of Ferry's boys rode waist--Norton.

Briol, October 27, 1944

We were briefed to bomb Mannheim today, the same target we bombed some time ago. We didn't fly, though, because of bad weather over Germany.   The mission was scrubbed before we left the ground.

There's a practice mission this afternoon but only the engineer and radio man are flying. We're going out to the range and practice with our .45 pistols. Hope I never have to use it but the German civilians are plenty unfriendly now and if we're forced down and get out alive, even the young German boys are armed with rifles and would start popping away at us at the drop of a hat.

I'm glad we didn't fly today. Got kind of a headache. I'm walking around half dazed lately. Never really had a headache before.

Briol, Saturday, October 28, 1944

There's a mission today but our crew is not flying.

We got in some more new crews. I'm worried about

some of these new crews. Some of them are right out of gunnery school with no operational training. Some of them haven't even had a high altitude mission before. It's not so good. I don't know what they'll do the first time they encounter enemy fighters.

This morning we went down to turret trainer and brushed up on our leading, tracking and framing enemy fighters in our sights. We'll probably get another prisoner of war lecture again. Our engineer and radio man are up on another practice mission.

I'm not sure yet about today's mission. We didn't go down to briefing. Maybe it's just a practice mission. Our crew is starting to compose themselves again. Instead of snapping at each other and brooding, we're starting to buck up again. Maybe it's because we have a lot of our missions behind us and if everything goes well, we'll soon be able to go home. The word home strikes a chord in my heart.

The mission today was to Munster, Germany. Our co-pilot (Welch) flew as tail gunner on a lead ship, so we were down at the line tonight sweating him out. He's okay. The ships weren't shot up very bad. A lot had feathered props. One cracked up on the runway but no one was hurt. The weather was foggy, wet and cold. I think we're going to a rest camp for our flak leave soon. We sure need it.

Welch Mission No. 18, Group Mission No 141, 28 October

The Group commander, Col. Rogner, requires that a copilot ride the tail gunner's position of the Group Lead airplane on each mission, to report on the rest of the formation in pilot's terms. The Lead can then make intelligent comments to the pilots of the remainder of the Group, concerning positions in formation, etc.

My turn was today, on a mission to Munster. The rest of our crew did not fly this one. Major Snow was the Group Lead, Air Commander. The gunners on the crew helped me get the guns installed, and briefed me on all the controls and switches in the position.

On climb out, I dutifully flashed the Aldis lamp out the tail while we were in clouds, then observed the formation coming into position on our wings, and reported to Major Snow on interphone. We joined the bomber stream over the Channel, still climbing. The view of the formation following us, and of the Groups coming along behind us, was marvelous.

I got busy getting my flak suit on as we approached enemy lines. I never did get it completely on. I wonder how Cornell, taller than I, ever manages to do it. The order came to test fire the guns, so I charged them a couple of times, then fired a short burst, aimed downward and to the side to miss the other airplanes in the formation. I was as ready as I could get.

As we got into enemy territory, the formation tightened up considerably, without one ship out of position. All the props I could see were turning. There was some flak at our level, off to one side, as we turned over the I. P. toward the target. The puffs were all ugly black, looked like 88's.

The target was socked in, so the bombs were dropped by Mickey-synchronized Norden bombsight. As we began our turn off target, flak behind us began creeping up on us, dead level. The black puffs plotted a pursuit curve on our tail, gaining steadily. I could feel the hair trying to stand up on the back of my neck; I tried to keep my voice calm as I reported it, while I prayed mentally.

Then, abruptly, we were out of range, the bursts fell behind us, then stopped. We began the slow upwind trip back to Glatton.

The oxygen check continued, but the crew could no longer hear my response. My running nose had built up an ice deposit over the mike in my oxygen mask. I finally realized what was wrong, and squeezed the mask several times, trying to break up the ice, but it still didn't work. So I turned partly sideways and gave the waist gunner the high sign that I was OK.

The rest of the mission was uneventful. I didn't even see a fighter other than our P-51's, much less shoot at one. Our crew's gunners, bless their hearts, met us to be sure I was OK

They even helped remove, clean and store the guns. What great guys! I love 'em.

Briol, Sunday, October 29, 1944

We didn't fly this Sunday. We were supposed to have a critique down at main briefing but I went to Mass instead over in our little base theater. May have a practice mission this afternoon. Weather has been pretty bad lately, probably slow down flying quite a bit. How I'm looking forward to that flak leave.

Welch, October 29, 1944

From time to time we carry different kinds of bombs. The usual, "standard" ones are 500 to 1,000 lb. General Purpose bombs (GP's).

A fragmentation bomb (Frag), usually weighing 250 lbs., is designed to explode on the surface or slightly above it, sending shrapnel fragments of its case in all directions.

An Incendiary Bomb (IB) is designed to ignite fires, by means of burning magnesium or other materials, thrown out all directions from the impact.

A special variation of the GP is the RDX bomb. Its explosive is much more powerful, and also much more sensitive to impact.

Each bomb has a small propeller on the nose or the tail, or both, which must revolve a certain number of turns before the bomb can explode at the desired point. Most explode on impact, though the GP may be fuzed to go off up to six days after it has penetrated the surface. These may be set off by any attempt to disarm them.

GP's and RDX's are used in trying to destroy railroad marshalling yards, bridges, oil refineries, factories, and so on. Frags are used against enemy troop concentrations. IB's are used against structures, vehicles, and so on.

RDX bombs, because of their sensitivity to shock, cannot be kept on board for landing. If not dropped in enemy territory, they must be jettisoned in the English Channel, away from surface craft.

Special safety wires, threaded through the fuzing propellers, keep the bombs from being armed until they are removed after take off. The little props spin after drop.

Bomb handlers get a little over-confident sometimes. One way of unloading GP's from a truck is to get up speed in reverse, then stop suddenly. The bombs roll harmlessly off the back of the truck. But that maneuver, used with a load of RDX's, blew up a whole bomb dump not too far from here.

Briol
Monday, October 30, 1944, Crew Mission No. 18
Group Mission No. 142

Our target for today was Munster. We didn't quite make it to the target today but we dropped our bombs on Germany, turned back, and it counted as a mission.

After we got over the Channel into Holland, there was some flak over the Zuider Zee as usual. No. 2 engine was squirting oil all over. We kept her going as long as we could to stay with the formation. It got so hot and vibrated so much we feathered it. No. 3 started smoking, and then No. 4. We were losing altitude and straggling.

We were almost over the German lines and decided we couldn't make it. We couldn't drop our bombs yet because our fighting lines were below. We couldn't go ahead alone over the target losing altitude. It would be duck soup for enemy fighters. We got over the Rhine into Germany, opened our bomb bay doors and let the bombs go, then turned around and beat it for the coast again. I don't know where the bombs hit. One bomb bay door wouldn't close, so it hung in the slip stream. We held our altitude pretty good then. We weren't attacked by the enemy but we were sweating it out. We limped back okay.

Harry, our tail gunner, is in the hospital, too, now. I think he'll be with us again soon, though. Another man flew tail gunner for us instead of Harry. Elliot flew waist again. I think we'll get Elliot permanently.

If we don't get that flak leave soon our whole crew will go to blazes. So far it was cancelled again. We were supposed to get it tomorrow.

We've flown every mission the 748th has put out, except three, since we started. Come to think of it, we even had to crank our landing gear down by hand today too, which is really labor.

It's almost getting to be a common thing to see the flak bursting around us. It's almost a common thing to see your buddies falling to a horrible death now but you can never get used to it. The flak crashes outside the plane and a thought flashes through my mind of the wonderful letters I received from Marcella and my folks, the day before, and I wonder how I'm ever going to see her and them again.

There were a lot of stragglers today. As far as I know one guy got the bends today, too, at high altitude. The temperature at 28,000 feet was about 50 degrees below zero.

The ship we flew today had just come out of the sub depot where it was being repaired for a long time after being crash landed, well, we put it back in sub depot again for a while. It needed some new engines, landing gear systems, bomb bay door systems and other things after today's mission. In spite of everything we have a darn good crew, what's left of it.

Spleth, Mission No. 19, October 30, 1944 (Monday)
#4 (591 W)
Target: Munster, Germany

Everything went O. K. Contrails started to give us quite a lot of trouble, however. About the time we hit Holland, #2 engine started losing oil. We kept in formation for a while, but soon started falling behind. We finally got our wing men to go ahead. We fell back and lost altitude, but managed to get to the I. P. We dropped our bombs just a few minutes after the I. P. and headed home by ourselves. We had lost quite a bit of oil. It was cold and the oil had piled up on the engine.

We had to crank our wheels down, and our bomb bays would not close.

#2 engine--internal failure.

Got credit for the mission.

Welch, October 30, 1944

Wedon's War Weary Willie (591 W) keeps on having troubles. The original engines were all changed out long ago. The British rebuilts just don't last long.

There continues to be a shortage of crews. Beginning with our first mission as a crew, the 457th Bomb Group has flown 22 missions in a period of 48 days. Our crew has flown 19 missions, not getting credit for one of them because of a mechanical abort. We're getting pretty tired, almost numb sometimes, and I think we've all lost weight. We miss a lot of meals, and are often too tired to eat after a mission. Square eggs and Spam are not the most attractive breakfasts, and every other meal seems to feature Brussels Sprouts. Byknish may be the lucky one, getting grounded when he did.

The shortage of crews has caused the tour requirement to be raised to 35 missions. Crew manning is supposed to be 15 crews per squadron. Also, they must be running out of medals. A crew member no longer gets a DFC when he completes his tour. He just gets an extra bronze oak leaf cluster on his Air Medal.

Briol, Tuesday, October 31, 1944

Our target for today was to be Politz again, right at Berlin, one of the worst hot spots for fighters and flak. The mission was scrubbed, though. After we worked our heads off early this morning in the cold and we were ready to takeoff, three red flares went up which meant we wouldn't takeoff. We may get it next mission. The largest and best part of our squadron died on the last raid to Politz. This would have been my third raid to Politz or Stettin.

Our squadron is built up strong now and this raid would have cut it to ribbons again. We were after the oil refineries there. They have one of the largest synthetic oil refineries in all Germany, and they really defend it. Our gas load was 2,750 gallons; 18 fragmentation bombs. Our route, same as the last raid there, would have been over the North sea, Baltic Sea and Denmark, down into Germany.

I can safely say that our losses over Germany have not been so bad lately for the damage we're inflicting on them. The trouble is, when there are losses, it usually falls on one group, such as fighter attacks, etc. I hope I have the worst part behind me. A man can't be sure. The psychological effects are always hard on the men, though.

Harry got out of the hospital today. I think he's okay again. He's a few missions behind us now.

Briol, Wednesday, November 1, 1944

Still no flying today. Just came back from main briefing where we had a flak lecture and current events lecture. This afternoon we have two hours of classes and skeet shooting. We cleaned and adjusted the guns on ship 591 again. The airmen always take care of their own guns because it's their lives at

100

stake. If a ground man took care of them he wouldn't care if they were all right or not. He doesn't use them.

Looks like it will be a long time before our flak leave. John Byknish is a little better but he'll never fly again. Just as we were going into main briefing, the Fortress, "Lady Luck" was landing. The landing gear buckled and she went crashing down the runway. The nose was smashed. The Ball Turret was squashed through the bottom and all four props corkscrewed as they beat into the ground. No one was hurt. It had been repaired and I think they were checking it.

We've never had a ship in one piece long enough to name it. We used "Lady Luck" on one mission before. We've flown "Lady Margaret" a few times. "Tarfu" was another ship we used.

I haven't handled the controls of a Fortress myself for a long time now. I had a chance on one of our last practice missions over here. I'm not as steady as I used to be.

Figure 13. 2/Lt. John Welch, 1944. (John F. Welch)

CHAPTER VII

BACK TO HELL AGAIN

Briol
Thursday, November 2, 1944, Group Mission No. 143

Today we "had" it again. I think I'll get credit for another fighter and damaged more. Our target for today was Merseburg. There was very little flak over the target but there were enemy fighters galore.

I'll skip most of it and tell about the fight. Like the Magdeburg raid we first saw the enemy off to one side. Nine o'clock this time. Our fighter escort was changing and they were nowhere to be seen which gave the enemy the chance they were looking for. They went around to six o'clock at our tail and began their "Company Front" attack. Our guns were blazing before the Jerries were even firing at us. Some of them turned off. The rest came right up, their cannons and machine guns blazing now. One of their 20 mm's ripped through our stabilizer exploding right next to the bomb bay filling it full of holes. Another went clear through our No. 1 engine without exploding.

I was blasting away at the nearest one again as he was coming up on us. I saw his prop and cowling go flying away and part of his wing tip go sailing behind him. He was out of control. The ship behind him, I think I damaged. Our tail gunner was also on him. He turned away smoking. Then, like last time our fighter escort was there and it seemed as if there were planes falling everywhere. I think we lost nine Fortresses.

This was somewhat like the Magdeburg raid. One Fortress exploded behind us. A man was thrown through the side and it looked as if he didn't have all his arms and legs. I saw two more Fortresses flaming but I think I saw most of the men get out. From now on, I'm afraid we'll have to expect fighter attacks on almost every mission.

It took one fighter attack to put our crew on the ball. Now, no matter how we hate to face them, we're always ready for them. It was after the attack when I felt like going crazy. My nerves were so strung, I didn't know if I was coming or going.

I got three shots of whiskey after we limped back and I felt much better. I might add, the ambulance was busy today, too. This sort of stuff doesn't come out in the newspapers but I imagine it will after the war.

When and if I finish my missions here, so help me, I'm going to get myself grounded. I can only take so much. They can bust me or anything else. They can even call me yellow if they want to.

The attack today lasted a few minutes but it went like lightning. I don't think we did a very good job of hitting the target.

Spleth, Mission No. 20, November 2, 1944 (Thursday)
#4, Lead box (394 N)
Target: Merseburg, Germany

Well, I was supposed to be stood down today. They had called the rest of the crews early from my hut, and there I was peacefully sleeping away. About 6:30 the CQ comes in and tells me I have to fly for Tweeten, who has suddenly taken ill. Eat breakfast and get out to the ship 30 minutes ahead of time and all are there but the ball turret gunner. He finally gets there and we get off.

Everything goes fine. We fly a lovely formation as we are expecting fighters. We get to the I. P. and before you know it we drop our bombs, and no flak. We find out later we were off course about 30 miles.

We make a right turn off the target and after a few minutes we are hit by fighters. About the same time we shuffle the deck with a low squadron. What a mess! Lots of planes were on fire and going down, both friendly and enemy. The attack was finally over.

We landed to find we had a 20 mm unexploded in our #2 gas tank. Had a 20 mm hit in the left horizontal stabilizer and (another in) #2 engine. No damage to the engine. Everyone O. K. Credit for two fighters.

Briol, Friday, November 3, 1944

Heavy ground fog today. It's drizzling, too. No flying.
I guess I was mistaken when I thought I had my worst

missions behind me. I'm afraid they're all ahead of me yet. I'm well over half way through with my missions.

We had a gunnery meeting this morning. For the Fortresses we lost on yesterday's mission, we must have shot down fifty enemy fighters, of course there are nine men to a Fortress too.

We must have lost about fifty Fortresses on this last raid. I think in all there were about 130 enemy fighters shot down by our Fortresses and escort fighters. We lost quite a few of our own fighters, too. It was a real hell with planes burning, exploding and falling everywhere. One enemy fighter out of control crashed into one of our Fortresses.

I can remember more now that it's all over. I didn't think much of it at the time but one of my shins is a little stiff yet from a small piece of 20 mm shrapnel that penetrated the metal in my ball and grazed my leg through my heated suit. It didn't tear any of the electrical wires, though. Sometimes when these wires are broken, they'll cause a short and start a fire. My Vickers unit was leaking oil all over me. Of course that happens quite often.

There were about 500 enemy aircraft in the air yesterday. These bad air attacks have started right after our crew started flying over here in the E. T. O. so we're getting it on all raids.

Got some good news again though. I think we get our flak leave on Monday the 6th.

When those blasted 20 mm's start exploding around you, for a second it looks just like flak.

I've often tried to figure out combat and although I'm in the thick of it, I can't explain it. More like some kind of dream. We fly over Germany with our bomb load and they blast at us from below trying to destroy us. Then their fighters come to try to destroy us and we fight back to destroy them before they destroy us. The important thing is to get our bombs to the target.

It gets in your blood. We talk combat, think combat, eat and sleep combat. You can't get away from it. When a crew is lost, the feeling is, he went down, somebody had to get it and it was he. We walk around and look at each other as much as to say, "Buddy, you're leading a dangerous life. Which one of us will be here tomorrow to enjoy life?" I don't know if you could call it an enjoyable life to be one step ahead of death. Back home I used to think of the fellows over here fighting and getting killed but man, I'm in it now and it's no fun.

In Germany they know almost every move we're making. By radar they know what we're doing from the time we take off and form over England to the time we're almost over the target. They don't know what target we're going to hit, though, at least they're not supposed to know. Usually, when there's a bad fighter attack something has slipped up. It takes them time to assemble and they have to know just where to hit us. Their fighters are of short duration and they can't stay up long. Our bombers form over England for hours sometimes, they fly all the way to the target, bomb, turn around and fly all the way back.

Our fighter escort can't make the whole trip either. One group escorts us and when they get low on gas another group takes over, (until the belly tank came out.) Germany is short on gas, too, we've bombed so many oil refineries.

Briol, Saturday, November 4

We just came down from a practice mission. No combat mission today. We found out that they dug a 20 mm projectile out of one of our gas tanks on the left wing from the last raid. If it would have exploded, it would have taken the wing off and sent us down in flames. Supposed to have an Army lecture for two hours this afternoon. We just flipped to see who would go down and sit through it and sign us in. Ozzie lost so he went down. Got little black kitten in here now. Having a lot of fun with it.

Had a fight in the hut today. Turned out kind of bloody.

May have to fly one more mission before our flak leave. Hoping we won't have to fly tomorrow and we'll be safe. We were supposed to have a 48 today but it was cancelled because of the flak leave.

The things we've seen on some of these missions could never be put into a movie. They can't make a movie horrible enough. I've never seen an air battle in the movies that could compare with some we've been in. Being in it and watching it are two different things. De Mille would have something to really talk about. They can't put this type of suffering in a movie. At least it isn't the same.

Briol
Sunday, November 5, 1944, Group Mission No. 144

Today, (Sunday) we bombed this marshalling yards in Frankfurt again. Took off early this morning but didn't land till late tonight because we hit mighty tough weather coming back. Our gas load was 2,800 gallons. Bomb load was six 1,000 lb. bombs. I put my little message from Marcy on the bombs again and watched them blow the marshalling yards and huge buildings sky high.

No fighter opposition today. The flak was intense, a solid wall. For a while I didn't think we'd get through it but we did. Got a few minor holes in the ship. The bomb bay and flap system were shot out and we had to labor with the hand crank again. They were really blasting us over the target but as I said, it didn't come to close to us. It hit the low and high box pretty hard. There were some casualties. One plane went down out of the low box and there were a lot of stragglers. We test fired our guns over enemy territory.

Even from our height I saw the marshalling yards and huge buildings being blasted and burning until the smoke hid the whole city from view.

Our crew seems to have a habit of coming through the most terrifying and intense flak, getting shot up pretty bad most of the time, but we manage to stay up there even if it's on one engine. This ship we used today (originally ours) won't fly for a long time again.

On the way back as usual we dodged most of the flak (evasive action) as we passed over Belgium, North Sea and on to England. When we hit the North Sea coming back, we dropped all the way down to 2,000 feet altitude, to get off oxygen and where it was warmer. Almost immediately we hit rough weather and fog all over England. Our base (Glatton) was all closed in. We searched around for two hours before we found a field.

During this time our Fortress was really thrown around. It seemed like everyone got air sick from it, except me. I don't even know what air sickness is like. I know it's pretty bad, Welch, our co-pilot, vomited right at the controls. Grybos vomited in the bomb bay. Harry was too sick to get to the bomb bay so he vomited in a chaff box in the waist. Just as we got into smooth air it left them. We landed at a field at last and went to chow there.

In a few hours it cleared up enough so we took off for our base. We got a bit of a scare on the way back. Our shot out bomb bay system started opening and closing the doors by itself. Then the electric motor in there started burning. We had packed away all our flying and heated equipment in our A-3 bags, including our parachutes. We weren't wearing any. I never thought I could get into a parachute so fast after zipping open the bag. Everyone dived for their bags at once. It was a dumb thing to pack away. The fire went out, though.

We're supposed to get our flak leave tomorrow. I'm going to get gloriously drunk, so is everyone else on our crew.

Spleth Mission No. 21, November 5, 1944 (Sunday)
#1, high element, high squadron (591 W)
Target: Frankfurt, Germany

Assembly O. K. and in to target O. K. Flak pretty heavy but evidently not too accurate. Bombs away O. K.

Assembled O. K. after bombs away. Left formation over Channel and started home with camera. Diversion message on way in. Landed at Ridgeway. Ate dinner and took off again after a couple of hours and came home O. K.

Before our first landing the air was as rough as I have ever seen it.

No battle damage.

CHAPTER VIII

BEAUTIFUL RESPITE

Briol, Tuesday, November 7, 1944

We got our flak leave yesterday. We're at a rest house at Worcester (Spechtley Park). It's in the western part of England. We got here yesterday afternoon. Had a short layover in Birmingham. Boy, what a place this is! This place is for the purpose of just getting rest and having a good time, to get our minds off fighters and flak. It's mostly run by women who act as sort of hostesses. We always get a double shot of whiskey before going to bed, and sleep as late as we like. Good food, always something to do and we'll get a whole week of it. It doesn't seem real. We had a dance last night, and I was drunk. In this game it's good for a man to get drunk, not at the wrong time, of course.

Today we had some archery. We can go hunting, horse back riding, etc. There are about 25 of us here. It's a huge English mansion built by Sir Robert Berkeley. It's a wonderful place, with tremendous rooms and staircases, and a big fireplace in every room. Deer heads hang over the fireplaces, etc. In the halls are knights' armor standing around, almost lifelike.

Right now we're all dressed in English civilian clothes and can stay dressed that way until we have to go back to that blasted hell in the air, but I'm forgetting that completely as long as I'm here.

Briol, Wednesday, November 8, 1944

Second day at the rest home. Having a lot of fun. Everybody and everything is swell, another dance last night. I'm sitting by the fireplace, getting ready to write some letters. It's raining out, and it looks like it will rain all day but it doesn't make a bit of difference.

It's funny how a person can go from one extreme to another. One day bloody fighting, and the next day living in a manor that you've heard about and seen but never dreamed of living in for a week. I feel mighty, mighty restless though. I detest going back to the job, and I'm mighty scared of it, but the sooner I get through with my missions the sooner I can go home.

A butler wakes us up in the morning. There are waitresses all over the place. A man just doesn't fit into this, but I'm not saying that I don't like it. Harry and Eddie came in drunk. Had to put them to bed. Last night when we were drunk our Top Turret gunner came out with the armor suit on. What fun!

Briol, Thursday, November 9, 1944

Third day at the rest home. Went to the stage play of "Rebecca" last night in Worcester. The cast came back with us after the play, and we sang songs, etc.

Briol, Friday, November 10, 1944

Fourth day at the rest home. Cycled down to a pub this morning. Shot some skeet. Went to a dance in town last night.

Briol, Saturday, November 11, 1944

A Lord and Lady visited us last night and had supper with us; stayed quite late. We watched a fox hunt this morning. It's quite interesting with all the hounds, the hunters in red uniforms, etc. Three of us went partridge hunting this afternoon (Ozzie, Tex and I) with some society. They're pretty nice about the whole thing. Their customs seem strange.

Tonight at supper one gunner was talking about the Magdeburg raid. He saw the group behind him get hit by fighters. He said he saw every plane in that box falling, flaming and exploding, except one or two. He thought it was horrible. Little did he know that those were our planes, and one of those two planes still flying was us, until I told him. I get goose pimples every time I think of it.

Briol, Sunday, November 12, 1944

Our last day here. We go back to flak and fighters tomorrow. It would be easier to shoot myself. I don't think I'm lying, either. It would really take less courage to shoot one's

110

self than to go out on some of those missions. What awful thoughts a man can get. Went to Mass in the morning at the chapel.

Briol, Monday, November 13, 1944

Spent most of the day traveling back to our base. Got back here about six tonight.

Welch, November 7 - 13, 1944

Courtesy of whomever, Spleth and I spent a delightful week at a "flak shack" for pilots at a country estate called Standbridge Earls, not far from Southampton. It's a great big country home that has been turned over to the British government for its use until the war is ended. Apparently most of the older servants are still there. It has lots of bedrooms, a stock of civilian clothes, and large, beautiful grounds.

We were wakened each morning by an elderly "gentlemen's gentleman", calling out "Wakey, wakey!" as he came around to each room, leaving a glass of juice for each guest. We then had an hour or so to get down to breakfast, which was typically British, and sure beat the heck out of the Mess Hall. After that we could choose from a variety of outdoor and indoor activities, punctuated by a good lunch and High Tea. Tea is tea, served with milk if you want it, but don't miss the scones. Our civvies weren't very formal and tailored, but it's sure no one cared.

There's a U. S. Army Hospital nearby, and we were invited there as guests of the nurses and doctors one evening. A GI truck took us to and from. When we walked in on arrival, everyone was handed a water glass of punch. It looked like and smelled like grape juice. One of the guys gulped his down and asked for another, quickly supplied. I took a couple of swallows and felt a warm sensation way down past my middle. It was spiked with medicinal alcohol (white lightning). I decided to go easy on that stuff. After we got "home" from the party, we had to partly drag, partly carry the guy who thought the punch was so good up a winding stairway to bed.

The next night, we invited the nurses to "our" place for a party. We had a good time visiting with the American girls. It fell to my lot, being almost sober, to ride along in the GI truck, and, following the passengers' directions, taking the guests back to their hospital quarters at Portsmouth. After we had left all the nurses at their places, we were uncertain about the way to go back, so we stopped at a sentinel post on the left side of the street to inquire. The gentleman on duty told us to continue ahead, turning right at every opportunity, and that would take us to the bridge back to the mainland.

"Y' cawn't miss it!", he said.

So we did as told, but became even more confused. Finally we pulled up to a sentinel post, on the right side of the street, and inquired again.

"Well, Blimey! Oi jist told ye! Y' cawn't miss it!" Same guard. We had missed it. But next time around we found it.

We've been talking to some of our "little friends", P-51 pilots, who have also been on flak leave. They have some hairy stories to tell, and take great pride in defending us, their "big friends". But we think one in particular has a doubtful sense of humor.

He told us he spotted a B-17 straggler on the way back from a mission, so he slid into forward formation position, where he got a "high sign" of O. K. from the pilots. He dropped back to look the rest of the airplane over, and saw that it had a hole in the waist he was sure he could have driven a Jeep through. But what he found very funny was that the waist gunner was running up and down the catwalk, beating himself with his arms, trying to keep warm. Not very funny to us.

On Sunday morning, we Catholics accepted an invitation to 8 a. m. Mass in a little church in the nearby town. We were back a little after nine, and enjoyed a late breakfast.

Spleth went with the Protestants to the 11 a. m. service at the Anglican church. When the service was over, they were asked to the Lord Mayor's house. As they walked in, each person was handed a small glass of wine. No one else was drinking it, so the Americans also waited. Finally the Mayor invited everyone's attention and proposed a toast.

"To His Royal Majesty, King George the Sixth!"

"To the King!" they all responded. The British guests each took a small sip of wine; the Americans turned their glasses bottoms up. And the Mayor proposed another toast,

"To his Excellency, the President of the United States, Mr. Franklin D. Roosevelt!"

112

"To the President!" they all shouted. But there stood the Americans with their empty glasses.

We enjoyed the rest of the day, complete with High Tea in front of the huge fireplace in the living room, and a very good dinner. And on Monday morning we put our uniforms back on and made our way back to Glatton.

All in all, it was a wonderful, relaxing week.

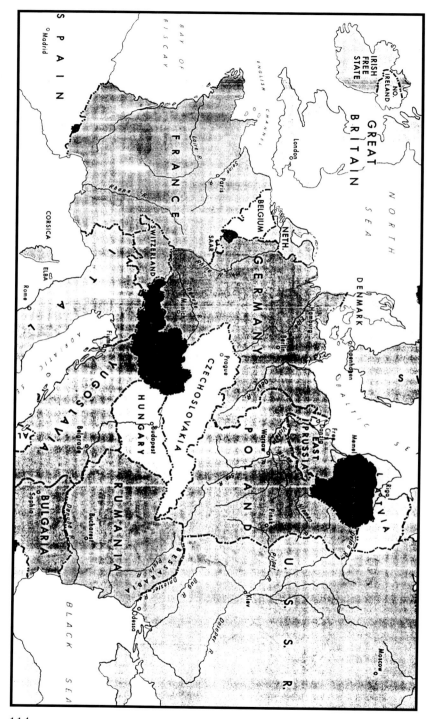

Figure 14. Map of Europe, circa 1944.

CHAPTER IX

BACK TO WAR

Briol, Tuesday, November 14, 1944

We briefed this morning to bomb the huge bridge at Bielefeld, Germany again. We didn't get to the target, though. We carried eight 1,000 lb. bombs. We got over the Zuider Zee in Holland and were called back. As we turned back and headed over the coast to the North Sea, the Germans on the coast sent up a bunch of flak barrages. We had dropped down to a few thousand feet.

Two of our ships met disaster here. We were all swerving around to evade the flak, when two Fortresses collided in mid-air. One ship broke right in half just back of the wing. The tail gunner was the only one who bailed out safely before it crashed into the North Sea below. We could see everything perfectly at the low altitude we were. It looked as if the tail gunner drowned because he didn't get free of his chute. The other plane that collided, although damaged, landed in the North Sea and ditched. We saw the life rafts pop out on the wings, then the men scramble out to the life rafts in the water and get in. The plane sank. The English didn't rescue them, we were too close to Holland. We saw the Germans coming out to get them.

I can still see men being thrown out of the plane that broke in half, with no chutes. I would have to see something like that right after a flak leave. Almost puts me back in the same shape I was in before the leave.

After we've been to one of these rest homes once, we can always go back for a visit on a pass. I'd like to go back on one of my passes soon. I kind of miss that place. Who wouldn't?

Briol, Wednesday, November 15, 1944

No mission today. We have a bunch of German prisoners working outside our hut. Guards watch them with rifles but we keep our .45's handy, too.

The wife of Legassa, (one of the men killed from this hut) has been writing to everyone who knew Legassa. I guess

115

she won't believe he's dead.

Briol
Thursday, November 16, 1944, Group Mission No. 148

We bombed the enemy lines today, just a little bit north of Aachen (Eschweiler). We passed over Aachen and it was really beat up. Our bombing (on the Belgium border) was to make way for another big push which will take place in a short time.

We must be the most shot at guys in the world. Our friendly troops were sending up short bursts of flak way below us as a marker, so we wouldn't bomb them. When we got over the enemy troops, their firing didn't even come close to us, although I saw thousands of guns blinking on the ground at us.

We carried 30 bombs, each 200 lbs. They were mostly small for killing troops, knocking out pill boxes, gun emplacements and ammunition dumps. I saw some huge explosions that were caused by ammunition dumps exploding. It wasn't easy, but it was very easy compared to some of the others we flew. Wave after wave flew over, but we were first.

We passed over the White Cliffs of Dover again after going over the Channel, then we ran into trouble. All of England was blanketed over with fog. We flew around for hours before we finally came in.

We narrowly missed hitting another ship in mid-air in the fog. We were almost out of gas. The fog was solid up to about a thousand feet. A lot of Belgium was blanketed with snow today.

We had to scrape snow and ice off the wings early this morning before we took off. We had one gas tank leaking all the way over Belgium. I thanked God when we were finally on the ground again.

I had my usual one meal before, that we get on the days we fly. We always get a carbohydrate (candy) ration but we don't enjoy it and don't get time to eat it.

I'm glad I didn't see any casualties among our men today but you can be sure the enemy had plenty.

We search our ships before takeoff for any stowaways because of these German prisoners around here. It has happened that they've stowed away in the camera well and before going

116

on oxygen, if they are armed will try to take over the ship and have it landed in German territory. They'll try anything, as I've seen. They aren't trespassing anymore, we're doing it now.

The cold was terrific as usual today. About 50 below. A man can't use much energy. It takes a lot of effort. A big man is at a distinct disadvantage on an aircrew. Maybe some day I'll appreciate the action I've seen from that Ball Turret. It's a terrible thing to appreciate, though.

The medics have us taking a sulfadiazine tablet every day. It's not too good for us while we're flying.

We're all tired tonight. The rest of the crew is asleep already. If I'm ever shot down this writing will probably be destroyed.

Spleth Mission No. 22, November 16, 1944 (Thursday)
 # 4, high squadron (591 W)
Target: Eschweiler, near Aachen, Germany

What an easy target. But what a day.

We took off with very poor visibility and then #3 gas tank had to start to siphon gas. After leveling off it finally quit.

We assembled O. K. and went over target O. K. Just friendly flak at lines. Came back to find visibility was not better. They stacked us up at 500' levels and called us in. We finally got in by making three passes at the field. No battle damage.

Only 12 of our 30 bombs went away. Bombing was supposed to be a huge success.

Briol, Friday, November 17

No flying today. It's so foggy you can hardly see the next building. We had a lecture this morning. We'll probably have some more classes today. We were highly complimented on the bombing we did yesterday. We wiped out a lot of men and equipment, in spite of the bad weather we had.

I still don't see how we managed to get on the ground safely. We couldn't even see the runway. We made about four passes at the runway before we finally made it.

I'll say one thing, It's not the pilots on the bombers who see and get the action. It's the gunners. Everyone has to work as a team. That's why it's best when the whole crew can stay together. So far we still have seven of our original crew. We're mighty fortunate. On many crews part of the crew goes down in battle, are hurt or broken up; anything can happen here.

It's raining cats and dogs now. There will be lots of days now that we won't be able to fly. It will be easier on us but we won't be able to go home so soon. There'll be icy runways and lots of extra worries. It seems like the temperature at high altitude couldn't get much worse but it will.

We finally got a write up in the paper on yesterday's bombing and it was really one of the easier missions for us. On some of the missions where a lot of us died, we hardly got a line.

Here's something I knew a long time ago. I noticed something of it in a paper. Combat men are usually in a state of shock, they call it, which makes a man sterile. It's only temporary though. It happens to every combat flyer.

A field, a few miles from here, was strafed by German fighters a couple days ago. I don't know how they got in and I don't know how they got out. It's kind of a mystery.

Briol, Saturday, November 18, 1944

It's still foggy and wet out. No flying. May go into Peterborough this afternoon. We have one class at one o'clock. Major just came through for inspection.

I heard that we killed off almost 200 out of 350 men in one company, when we bombed day before yesterday. If we die now, we've sure made up for it.

The floor of our little chapel is flooded with mud and water. We have to stand up in there now.

It's still raining quite hard. I heard the song, "There's a Star Spangled Banner Waving Somewhere" for the first time in a long time today. That song almost brings tears to my eyes every time. I don't know why.

Welch, November 20, 1944 (Monday)

Airplane Crew Chiefs and mechanics are the main reason we can keep up our bombing effort. We arrive back from a mission with the airplane shot full of holes, needing everything

118

from patches to new wiring to engine changes, and they go right to work on it, regardless of weather. Unbelievably, the airplane is ready to go on another mission the next morning. 591 W's ground crew is fantastic; we don't see how we've been able to fly it as many times as we have.

The mechanics are on the same rations, etc. that we are, but live in tents. Spleth and I don't smoke, so we always give our line men our rationed cigarettes. While we're trying to get some sleep for the next day's mission, those guys are toiling through the night to provide us with the best possible airplane for the next day's effort. They deserve a whole handful of some kind of medals.

Briol
November 21, 1944, Tuesday

The target for today was Merseburg again (but we didn't fly).

On these missions I'm on the alert every second for enemy fighters. It makes a man awful tense. Your eyes hurt when the white clouds below reflect the sunlight. I search 360 degrees at all times. If something happens I usually see it. It doesn't do me any good to see some things.

I haven't counted the missions I have written up here. I think there were some first ones I didn't write up. About three, I guess. There were some we didn't get credit for. Couldn't talk operations into it.

We lose men and planes all right but it's nothing compared to the terrible havoc we cause the Germans below. It's really something to see huge entire cities burning and blowing up, especially Berlin. There are other smaller cities in Germany that are of much greater importance than Berlin, though, such as industries, refineries, marshalling yards, etc.

Welch, November 21, 1944

We've had some crew conversations about what we should call our crew, and what to get painted on the backs of our A-2 leather jackets. With more than 20 missions in, we seem to be behind, somehow.

A few days ago we were batting around some possible

names, and someone suggested we call ourselves "The Dead End Kids". Trying to be funny, I said that, considering our record with airplanes, it would be more appropriate to call ourselves "Dead <u>Engine</u> Kids". To my surprise, the idea was snapped right up, and so we finally have a name, "Dead Engine Kids".

The picture will show a B-17 flying with one engine feathered. When (if?) we finish our tour, underneath the picture will be "35!", to indicate 35 missions flown.

The gunners know a man who can do the painting, so when he's ready I'll turn my jacket over to them to get the job done. I think he charges only about a pound.

Briol, Wednesday, November 22, 1944

No flying today. Last night it rained all night and it's foggy as the dickens today. From now on we're going to form our formations over France because the weather is always bad over England now. We'll always take off here, climb above the weather, head for France on our own and meet the rest of the ships there, and then on to the targets in Germany. We're going to get a 48 hour pass sometime this afternoon. I'm just going to Peterborough and sleep at the Red Cross. I'll just mess around and maybe I'll drown my sorrows in an English pub.

Briol, Friday, November 24, 1944

We spent our whole pass in Peterborough. Our group flew one mission to the Ruhr Valley while we were gone. I hear it was a milk run, so to speak.

In Peterborough we spent most of our time at the Red Cross. We slept there and had Thanksgiving supper there. The supper was pretty good if I do say so myself. Went to a dance at Du Jon's Cafe. A lot of Polish paratroopers in town.

Ozzie went to London again. He isn't back yet. He wanted to get his jacket painted. I do too.

I saw in Stars and Stripes a case where a Fortress on a raid had been shot up and it was going to crash land. The Ball Turret gunner was trapped in the ball and couldn't get out. Everyone got orders to bail out but the pilot, waist and tail gunners stuck with the trapped ball gunner. They were all killed. The story was told by the men who bailed out. I don't ever want anyone to stick by me if they have a chance to save themselves. I had to crank myself out of a ball once when the electrical system went out. It takes a lot of effort.

There was a beauty contest at the Aero Club tonight for some of the English girls who come down here. Father Ludder was one of the judges, believe it or not.

Welch, Friday, November 24, 1944

An Aviation Cadet classmate of mine, Porter B. Whittier, flies B-24's out of a base over by Norwich. I decided to go visit him on my 48-hour pass. When I got over there, several hours and several trains later, he was out on a mission. So I went and spent a couple of hours in the Norwich Castle Museum, then went to the Red Cross to get a room for the night. The lady asked to see my special pass from my base adjutant. I didn't have one. So I caught a ride out to the nearest U. S. Army Air Base, and spent the night there. It was nice, formerly a permanent RAF base.

This morning I went to ask the Base Adjutant if he could fix me up with a special pass. He told me there's a special deal on, to pick up people who are deserters, AWOL or spies, walking around in U. S. Army uniforms, and he should turn me in, since I don't have a special pass from my Squadron Adjutant. After some negotiation, he consented to give me a special pass authorizing me to be away from his base, but I could use it only to go back to Glatton. So I didn't get to see P. B. After the complex cross country by train from Norwich to Peterborough and Glatton, I find out that it would be a lot quicker to go by way of London.

When I read the 748th Squadron Bulletin Board this evening, there was a notice which said that anyone going on pass over this period has to go by the Orderly Room to pick up a special authorization to be away from the base. Welch, let that be a lesson to you--read the Bulletin Board every day.

Briol
Saturday, November 25, 1944, Group Mission No. 151

Our target for today was Merseburg again. I think we

really polished it off this time. We briefed early this morning and didn't get back until late tonight. Our gas load was 2,700 gallons . We carried twelve 500 lb. GP bombs for each plane.

I saw only one Fortress go down in flames today but the sky was full of stragglers. The enemy fighters didn't get through to us. Our ship didn't have a single hole in it, thank God. Because there were enemy fighters in the area, every straggler had one or more of our fighters protecting it. We came close to colliding with another ship on the way to the target. He hit some prop wash and was thrown straight down right in front of our nose almost crashing into us. The ship headed straight down in a dive for about 2,000 feet. It finally pulled out and climbed back into formation. It was close.

At the target I never saw so much flak in my life, even worse than Politz was. It seemed to be all the way from 18,000 to 30,000 feet. It ranged for almost a ten mile area. Still we went through it without getting a hole. Things like that don't just happen. I couldn't figure how we heard those tremendous whumps and being thrown around and still not get blown to bits. They couldn't see where they were shooting because there was a cloud coverage, so they had to use radar and we disrupt their radar with chaff.

For the second time now we also used a new radar weapon. The ships are being installed with them now. We turn them on in the ship and it messes up the German radar waves and they can't shoot straight from the ground when there's a cloud coverage. God knows, they come close, though, and get direct hits. My fire cut off switch stuck (froze) today when I test fired my guns in enemy territory. I had to fix it. The crew was sweating me out because the belly of the ship is the weak spot and my guns are the only ones that protect it.

It was about 50 degrees below zero. When we descended into warmer air there was a thick coat of frost on all the metal. My left heated glove went out and I had to get one out of the extra A-3 bag before I froze my hand.

Our course was through Belgium, north tip of France into Germany, same way out. Coming back over the fighting lines, we watched the huge guns and shells exploding.

Hitting the coast of England we passed over the White Cliffs of Dover again. Then we ran into the usual English fog and had the usual close calls and sweating out the landing. By the time we landed, it was late and dark.

When I get through with these missions I'm going to quit flying, so help me. Got my usual shot of whiskey which hit the spot, then my first meal all day. I don't know how this flying is for the appetite. Your stomach expands terribly (that is, the gases, etc. expand), and when you come down it shrinks. I've come to the conclusion man wasn't made for this sort of life. I've heard the expression "scared to death", well, I believe now that a man can be so scared that he'll die from it after a while. If a man had to stay at this job too long, there's no telling what could happen.

Spleth, Mission No. 23, Group Mission No. 151, Saturday
November 25, 1944, #4 high box (591 W)
Target: Merseburg, Germany

Not much to this mission. We naturally sweated out a scrub, but no sale. We had good Division formation all the way in.

Bombardier dropped on lead box #3 ship, who salvoed. What a deal--we dropped too early.

Flak was not bad, came home O. K. Visibility down to about ??, ceiling 300 feet.

No battle damage.

Briol
Sunday, November 26, 1944, Group Mission No. 152

We briefed early this morning (Sunday) to bomb Misburg, a few miles from Hannover, Germany. Our ship didn't get to the target though. We aborted before we got to the coast of Holland. Our No. 1 engine went out on us and threatened to burn. We couldn't keep up with the formation. We were pretty low and had turned around and were heading back for England. We dropped our bombs in the Channel to get rid of the hazard and the weight. I watched them explode when they hit the water. A geyser of water shot high into the air. We scared the fish, anyway. They probably heard it back in England. We carried twelve 500 lb. bombs.

This will give me a chance to go to Mass this afternoon. We've finally got a permanent waist gunner again, named

Lambertson. He has in about half the number of missions we have. His crew was shot down one day he didn't go along. Pretty nice fellow! He's on the ball, too.

There's a lot of beefing about the cigarette shortage. We combat flyers still get our five packs a week. I smoke more than that, though. Three men on our crew who don't smoke buy theirs and give them to us who smoke, so we're pretty well fixed. The ground crew and men don't get any at all now.

I think all our ships got back from today's raid, though some were shot up a bit. We were briefed to destroy the natural oil refineries at Misburg. It was completely camouflaged. After studying the photographs and close ups, we could pick out everything, although it was clever.

Maybe it's a good thing we had to turn back today. I'd have probably had a frozen hand. My right heated glove went out and there was no extra in the bag. I didn't say anything. I was going to stick it out. It was 50 below.

Coming back from Merseburg yesterday, I took special notice of the Rhine River and its surroundings in Germany, just before we went over the fighting lines. It is an awful rugged country around the Rhine. Our troops are going to have it mighty rough there. It's hilly and treacherous. There are tremendous slopes going down to the Rhine. It winds and curves. There were cities and villages burning around the fighting lines. You could see dust, smoke and the guns flashing. Boy, what pictures I could have taken on these missions! I have taken some pictures from the ball but it was a course of duty, such as bombs away and the bombs hitting the target. They're turned in to intelligence. We don't do it every time. When our turn comes they come down to the ship and install the movie camera before we take off. I don't like it because I'm too busy. Otherwise a few ships in each group take pictures from a camera installed in the camera well in the radio room.

I found out the Luftwaffe was up after us again today. Although they didn't hit our squadron, they shot down 39 Fortresses. Our Fortresses and fighters got 110 of them. (49 Fortresses in two days lost).

Spleth, Mission No. 24A, Group Mission No. 152
Sunday, November 26, 1944, #4

Target: Misburg, Germany

Fonnesbeck (?) leading.

Assembled O. K. We got out about 10 minutes from English coast and #1 oil pressure dropped and oil temperature went up, oil started coming out of breather. So we dropped out of formation, dropping our wheels, and attempted to feather. Some (slowing) but motor burned out, prop was windmilling. So we dropped our bombs in Channel and came home. We had plenty of oil (30 gallons) so engine did not freeze up. Mechanical abort.

Briol, Monday, November 27, 1944

We briefed to bomb Frankfurt this morning. The mission was scrubbed because of weather. We had our guns all in and everything ready to go. This sort of thing happens pretty often now.

This morning we were sending out twelve extra Fortresses to drop chaff near to the target before we went over to bomb it. Those planes would be the first over. They don't have to hold a steady course, so they can evade flak. It's different when you're bombing. You have to keep coming straight through the flak.

We had mutton for chow tonight. The blasted stuff gags me even when I'm hungry.

So far since I have arrived here, no crews have finished their missions or gone home from this squadron. On the Magdeburg raid a lot of our new and old crews were annihilated. From what I've seen, however, normally it seems to be the crews that have from one to five missions go down. If a crew gets in above fifteen missions it seems as if they have a pretty good chance. I'm planning on making it although sometimes my faith looks hopeless.

I wish I'd have been here a few months earlier when there weren't so many attacks by enemy fighters. When so many fighters gang up on a small group of bombers, no matter how good the gunners are, a couple passes and the group will be wiped out.

Of course, they are sending strong fighter escorts with us now, but like Magdeburg, the escort often scurries off to intercept the enemy and another group of enemy fighters attacks the bombers. They usually attack the low box first, then sweep up to the lead and high box. We were in the low box at Magdeburg, where everyone was wiped out except two of us. Everything happened so fast before, I didn't have much time to think about it. Now I'm so grateful I don't know what to think.

Welch, November 27, 1944 (Monday)

In places in our Squadron area, the dirt is washed away from the edges of the concrete pavement down as much as six inches. With only a little light from my flashlight, I ran off the edge of one of those places with my bicycle on the way to briefing for a mission to bomb Frankfurt this morning. The bicycle wasn't hurt, but my right ankle was. Now I can't walk; my bicycle is my only way of getting around. I didn't tell anybody, because I didn't want to miss flying with the crew, and thought I could sit in the airplane O. K.

After the mission was scrubbed, I went to see the Flight Surgeon. He said nothing is broken, and it is going to swell up and hurt like hell. (I already knew that last part). He offered to ground me, but I want to be able to fly if the crew does, so I declined.

Though I'm kind of wounded, I can't blame it directly on enemy action, so I don't qualify for a Purple Heart.

Briol, Tuesday, November 28, 1944

No flying today. It's still foggy and raining out. These missions are going to be a long drawn affair now. We had classes all day which bored me to death. We had a dental check, too. Couldn't find anything wrong with my teeth. Of course, they don't try very hard. I think our crew will fly at five o'clock this afternoon to take some navigators somewhere.

I got two letters today. The first I got in two weeks.

So far we haven't had a plane whole, long enough to name it. We had a ship assigned to us but we put it back in sub depot again, where it's getting a new engine. It was a new ship but it is ready for the junk heap now. One thing I like about it, it's one of the fastest ships in the formation.

If I should go down, I've fixed it with a ground man, to

take this writing to the States. I'm foolish to ever want anyone to read this stuff but I guess I want someone to know what the bomber crews do over here. It isn't exactly a thumb twiddling contest.

Welch

Operations decided that our crew needed a night practice mission for proficiency, so on a very dark and cloudy evening, away we went, flying at about 9,000 feet. We headed South, toward London for a while, but turned West when we heard "r-r-r-R-R-R-r-r", a siren sound, on our command radio. It was the warning signal from the barrage balloons around London.

These balloons are tethered in a ring around London, to fend off German bombers. Each balloon has cables hanging from it. At intervals along each cable are high explosives, set to go off on contact. If an airplane flies into a cable, it will drag over the surface of the wing or tail until one of the charges hits the surface, which is then blown to bits. The balloons carry low power transmitters putting out the siren sound on the UK universal air command frequency, and can be heard when within the standard range of about ten miles; fair warning to friendly pilots.

The black out of the ground below was complete, we couldn't see any lights at all on the ground or in the air around us. We might as well have been in an ink well. But suddenly there were blue exhaust flames in all directions. We had blundered into an RAF bomber stream of some sort. We turned every light in and on the airplane to as bright as it would go, hoping they'd at least see and avoid <u>us</u>.

We decided to test the emergency going-home system; it's supposed to respond and show us the way to go. So we said on the radio (limited to ten miles range),

"Hello, Darky, Hello Darky!"

On the radio we heard in response,

"Aircraft calling Darky, go ahead with your request."

"Darky, this is Wedon W William, please show us the way to go home,"

"Roger, Wedon W William."

All at once, ahead and to the left, a searchlight aimed straight up into the sky, then lay over to a horizontal position.

We flew along in the direction it was pointing, and began a slow descent toward our traffic pattern altitude. Presently it went off and another ahead of us pointed straight up, then lay over horizontally. We followed the directions pointed until finally, out in front of us, we saw a ring of dim lights a couple of miles across. We turned to follow left hand traffic around it. (These are called perimeter lights.) Presently we saw a funnel of lights leading off to the left and turned into it. The perimeter lights went off behind us, and we descended to final approach altitude. Shortly the runway lights came on in front of us, and the funnel lights went out. We landed successfully and slowed to taxi speed. Then the runway lights went out, and we had nothing but our landing lights to find our way to our hardstand. Clever people, these British.

Briol, Mission No. 22
Wednesday, November 29, 1944, Group Mission No. 153

Our target for today was Misburg again. This time our plane did not carry bombs, but a bomb bay full of chaff instead. We were one of a box of twelve ships that led the whole 8th Air Force over the target. We were the screening force. We all carried chaff except the lead ship, which had bombs and dropped them on a minor target on the way over.

This job is more dangerous than carrying bombs, in some ways. There are only twelve ships, so we would be duck soup for enemy fighters. We had good escort fighters, though.

We don't have to go directly over the target, so we can evade some of the flak. Our job is to drop this chaff near the target so when the rest of the bombers get to the target the enemy's radar is all messed up and they can't get the range of the bombers to shoot them down. Most of their shots go wild then. There was flak all the way in and out. We evaded most of it. After we dropped our chaff we circled the target as the first group of bombers came over. The Germans were firing away but our chaff did a good job. As the first group left the target we cuddled up to it for protection and started back.

We had splendid fighter protection today. P-51's, P-38's and P-47's and lots of them. In briefing we were told 750 enemy fighters were expected to be waiting for us. They never got through to us. They were up but our fighters were on the ball. Many were strafed and destroyed on the ground. I saw a few enemy fighters go down.

We used another ship this morning because ours is still in sub depot. The crew that landed this ship the last time, let the Ball Turret come out of stowed position while landing and the guns hit the runway. It messed things up a bit and I sweat my brains out getting it into firing condition, before takeoff. I wasn't going into fighter territory with poor guns.

It was cold on the ground early this morning. It was about 45 below at altitude. Our gas load was 2,500 gallons per ship. Our course after we left the English coast was over the North Sea, Dutch coast, Zuider Zee, Holland and into Germany. It was the same route out again. The flak guns were blasting away at us all the way until we finally got over the North Sea again. We used a lot of evasive action. We got through without a hole in our ship.

Got back in time for 5:30 Mass. Ate chow and now I have time to jot this down before hitting the sack. I was turned away with a low heart at the mail room. No mail, going on the third week now. Christmas rush!

Swiped some bread and butter at the mess hall and took it back here and made some toast. Eddie and I often do that.

I was so tired today after we landed that I could hardly put my equipment away. There wasn't any whiskey for us today.

Spleth Mission No. 24B, November 29, 1944 (Wednesday)
#4, only box
Target: Misburg, Germany

Chaff unit, what a nice deal. We assembled O. K. and started out. We made a nice 360° East of Zuider Zee and picked up nice fighter support.

We skirted the target area and dished out our chaff.

Our squadron leader drug us through all the prop wash in the country on the way back, but will trade it for flak any day.

Landed O. K.

Welch, November 29, 1944

A very eerie thing happened on a late morning takeoff a

while back. For a change there were only a few high clouds, and the dawn was quite beautiful in the East, with the sun about to come up. Then, rising vertically, we saw two shiny vapor trails. We knew right away that they were made by German V-2's, those rockets they've been dropping in on London.

Radar probably doesn't pick them up, and even if it did, there's no way of stopping them. They go very high, and then fall in on the target. Since they fall in going faster than the speed of sound, they can't be heard coming. They're said to contain more than a ton of explosive, so they do a lot of damage. How accurate they are doesn't make a lot of difference when they're aimed at a city the size of London.

The V-2's are the reason Lauren Spleth and I don't go to London any more.

CHAPTER X

THE WAR IS NOT OVER

Briol, Mission No. 23, Thursday, November 30, 1944
Group Mission No. 154
December 2, 1944 (Saturday)

I've got quite a tale to tell again tonight and it's not exactly nice to talk about. We took off early in the morning of November 30th, 1944, and didn't get back to our base till late tonight. We had to crash land in Belgium, but our whole crew is safe.

Our target for that morning was Bohlen, Germany, way on the other side of Germany right next to Leipzig. It was over Leipzig where most of our planes were blasted out of the sky after we hit the target.

We were briefed to run into 800 enemy fighters at the target but they didn't get through our escort. Our gas load was 2,750 gallons. We carried twelve 500 lb. bombs.

So people think the war will be over by Christmas! If they only knew how rough and horrible it is. There was a movie camera installed in my Ball Turret this time and it was my turn to try to get pictures. I got some good ones although I don't think I care to see them.

In all I think there were 58 bombers shot down. There were seven Fortresses shot down out of our box of twelve ships. I saw almost every one go down.

I was scared sick all the way over on this mission. We were prepared for the enemy fighters. Man, how we were sweating this one out. We got some flak all across Germany but it wasn't too accurate. The ships were starting to stream vapor trails. We were nearing the target after hours over Germany. Ahead I could see the flak over the target and Leipzig. Man, oh, man! Miles and miles of it. As we got closer the group in front of us went over the target. I turned my ball up in position and flipped the camera switch to take a movie of the flak.

Just as I flipped the switch, there was a huge, tremendous explosion in the flak as a B-17 and all its crew blew to smithereens. There wasn't even a piece left to see. It was a merciful death.

Their bombs exploded right in the plane. I had the whole thing in the camera.

I had taken some more pictures before that of the vapor trails, the formation and some B-17's straggling. One plane dropped its bombs before it got to the target. I got them exploding on one end of a little village on film.

My main orders were to get a picture of our bombs falling and where they hit.

As we neared the target, I got a picture of the fires and explosions below but we didn't drop our bombs even though we went over the target. Our Colonel, the base commander, was leading us. No one dropped their bombs because he didn't drop his. He ordered us to do a 360 degree and go around again and make another run on the target. Very few ships were lost on the first run but the second run was disastrous.

He wasn't satisfied, but thanks to him, we lost a lot of ships. His ship was crippled a little by flak on the first run, so he didn't make the second run but ordered the deputy lead to do it. He started heading back while we went over the target again.

Then and there I never saw such horrible flak in my life. There were tremendous, stunning explosions all around us. Fortresses started flaming, exploding and falling all around us. I was praying out loud again.

There were terrific flashes and concussions. Wham! and most of our No. 1 engine was blasted away. The prop was still there windmilling and throwing fire. We were directly over the target. The ship started nosing down a little. We got a terrific jolt. I think Spleth was stunned because Welch took over the controls in the co-pilot's seat.

The bombs went away and my orders were to get those pictures of them going down to the target. I got them but not to the target because clouds got in the way.

Ozzie called for an oxygen check. Everybody's voice was shaking. Our formation was spread all over the sky and there weren't many ships left. We ran into most of the flak over Leipzig and we only had three engines now.

There was red hydraulic fluid leaking out of the cockpit and it looked like blood. We thought Spleth was hit and bleeding.

Our ship was still jumping like a jackrabbit as the flak burst. It seemed like we were in it for hours but I think it was about fifteen minutes. Before we got out of it, a piece of flak

132

went through the nose right through Ozzie's parachute on his back. It saved his life.

There were a couple heavy thumps in the wings and gas started leaking. Spleth took over again. One rudder control was shot away. A piece of flak came through the radio room right in back of Eddie's neck. He was bent forward and it missed him. One of the oxygen tanks exploded and one system started getting low on oxygen. Our radio, liaison and command, was shot away. A big piece of flak came through the waist and through a couple of our bags with equipment in them. Our navigator's shoe was grazed by one piece. One piece thudded against my Ball Turret but the guns saved me. It hit the receiver on one gun.

Our G-box burned out. Our flaps and landing gear control systems were shot away.

We were straggling far behind the rest of the planes now and slowly losing altitude. We were afraid of being attacked by enemy fighters. We used flares to try to get some of our fighters to protect us but no luck. We couldn't radio for help. No radio. Once again we were all alone over enemy territory. Our fighters were still around somewhere, so the enemy didn't get to us.

We were about in the center of Germany now and limping along. We were getting low on gas. All of a sudden that windmilling prop set up a terrific vibration. I got out of the ball and into my chute, changed oxygen connections and other connections.

It wouldn't be good to bail out over Germany. We were all ready, though.

I don't see how the ship hung together. The wings were flapping up and down almost a foot. We couldn't keep our feet on the floor. I was praying out loud under my oxygen mask again. The vibration stopped a little and we finally got over the fighting lines into Belgium, with very little gas left.

We decided to crash land at an air field we spotted through the clouds because we figured we had a good chance. We got the gear and flaps down by hand; no brakes. We braced ourselves and came in. We went off the runway and sheared off a post of some sort. The prop on No. 1 went flying. The waist door flew off. But we made it. I had taken the camera out of the ball.

We came down in an air field. It was a P-47 fighter base. (9th Air Force). We were all pretty well dazed.

They treated us swell over there. We got our bags and equipment out of the ship by truck. We caught a bunch of guys stealing all our stuff. We were in no pleasant mood after our ordeal, so we promptly got it all back with our .45 pistols. We got most of it back anyway.

We found out we had come down just south of Brussels, near the city of Mons. We actually enjoyed our stay immensely. Everyone talks French there. Our navigator could speak French, so we got along pretty well. The women are nicer and neater than the English, although we can't understand them.

I never take any ID or money along, except dog tags, etc. They don't give us the kits any more with French money but our navigator had plenty money. He changed it to Francs. He loaned me 1,000 francs which would be six pounds in English money or $24 in American money. We ate chow at the fighter base. We were waiting for a C-47 transport plane to pick us up.

A lot of the buildings were still wrecked. The Germans used to have that base. Bomb craters were all over. German sign posts and posters were still there. There were some German cars there too, that were captured and the Americans were using. They drive on the right side of the road in Belgium like the Americans.

I didn't see any soap or warm water all the time I was there. We didn't shave, so we looked like tramps, walking around with our pistols strapped to our hips. They're very nice to Americans in Belgium. The English stink.

They took us to Mons in a truck and we slept in the Espercon Hotel. The next day we walked around and looked things over, went to the fighter base and ate chow. They have hardly any food in Belgium but they have good beer and wines, etc. We ate breakfast in Mons at the E. M. quarters.

Our C-47 hadn't come in yet so we went back to Mons again. That night we went to a dance there. We kind of drowned our sorrows, too. That night we slept in the Grand Hotel, the best hotel in Mons. They're pretty lenient with Americans. Some of the crew slept at the Mille Cologne.

Some outhouses are public. They don't separate men and women. It's something Americans can't get used to.

134

They have lots of strange customs. The men going to school come marching down the streets arm in arm in a long line, singing, hollering or shouting. Most of the streets are brick. They're pretty clean about their streets and sidewalks. Every morning the women are out there scrubbing and cleaning the sidewalks. We had some toast and coffee at the E. M. quarters for breakfast, then we went shopping. I didn't get much, a piece of jewelry for 150 francs and some handkerchiefs for 75 francs.

We went back to the fighter base to wait for our C-47 transport. We finally had to fly to France in the transport to a C-47 base. From there we got a C-47 back over the Channel to England.

They had our clothes salvaged here at the base already but we got them back. We're going to get a physical tomorrow, I guess, to see if we can still take it, then we're going to get a three day pass to let the ordeal wear off.

Zeiler's crew made it all the way back, so we're still together in this hut. They had given us up.

Before I forget it, that P-47 base in Belgium used to be a German JU-88 Bomber base. There's still a bomber graveyard full of wrecked German planes. I got a few parts for souvenirs.

The extra two men left in this hut from Flannery's crew had to bail out over Belgium. I think they're safe but they're not back yet.

Spleth Mission No. 25, Group Mission No. 154
November 30, 1944, Lead High-high (583)
Target: Bohlen, Germany

Assembled and proceeded to target area. Target was covered so they made a 360 to left. The Colonel had to feather an engine and dropped out of formation.

We got hit on second run, first up under the instrument panel, then in #1 prop dome, causing it to run away, and loss of oil. Eventually it froze, causing the guts to break loose. Vibration was terrific--don't see how the wing stayed on.

Hydraulic line was also shot away. We got into friendly territory without any more flak or enemy fighters. We were very low on gas, 85 gal. in 3 tanks when we were somewhere over Belgium.

Oh! Yes--G-Box went out on way in to target, caught fire. We came over a clear spot in the undercast and saw a nice juicy P-47 base. Made a poor visibility landing, losing prop (#1) and main door. Ground looped plane to right. Had a nice stay.

Came home Dec. 2, in a C-47 first from Base 84 to 35, and then to 130.

Ozenberger Mission No. 23, November 30, 1944

A very rough mission was to Bohlen, Germany the 30th of November. We came back to the ground by the grace of God. No one else could have done it.

Bohlen is just five miles from Leipzig. Leipzig has twice as much flak as Berlin. We went all the way to the target and everything was O. K. We went down the bomb run and over the target and didn't get any flak. Not that there wasn't any, but we were just out of range of it. There were no bombs dropped and we started around for a 360°.

The first time over we lost three or four planes, they were out of the lead and low boxes. The next time over our high box was the only box that was in formation, so they really gave it to us. I don't know where they got so much flak.

We really got it; our No. 1 engine got a direct hit and broke loose. Flak came through the nose, and scraped along Braffman's leg and went up through the controls. A piece broke the rudder pedal off from under Spleth's foot. Another cut the hydraulic lines. Another ripped and tore all the instruments in the cockpit, and another one hit me in the parachute. I felt the thud when it hit.

A lot of flak hit in the radio room, waist and tail, also some in the cockpit. One came through the radio room and missed Grybos' head by two inches. Inasmuch as we had no rudder, we had a hard time turning out of the range of the flak. We thought we were out of it three times, but each time they started shooting at us again. All three times they hit us.

In trying to turn out of the flak and start home again, we made too large a circle which was due to not having a rudder, and slid over into the Leipzig flak and had a taste of it, too.

By the time we were at last out of the flak and on our way home, the rest of the planes were almost out of sight, so once more we were left alone. The No. 1 prop was vibrating so much that I couldn't sit on my seat in the nose. The prop was not only vibrating, but it was wobbling so much that it was cutting up the engine, due to the fact that it had broken loose from the crank shaft, and nothing was holding it in the engine except the force of the wind; so as it turned (also due to the wind), it ate its way back into the engine.

Some way we had lost a lot of gas and knew we couldn't make it back to England. We finally found an opening in the clouds and went down through it, hoping that when we got within sight of land that it would be out of Germany. Not that we could tell by the sight of the land, but we were praying for it anyway. After we came through the clouds, we saw an air field in the distance. We didn't know what it was, but we knew we had to go down, what ever it might be.

It turned out to be a P-47 field of an advanced fighter group. It was just 25 miles back of the front lines. We messed up the field a little when we landed, but were sure glad to be on the ground. Spleth and Welch made a good job of landing it when they had nothing to work with, inasmuch as everything that they were used to using in landing had been shot out.

Once again no one was hurt. We stayed in Belgium for a few days, flew to France in a C-47 then on to England in another one. In France we picked up another crew that had been shot down from our same base, and we all went back to England together.

Welch, Mission No. 24, Group Mission No 154,
November 30, 1944

This was my 24th mission. The target was a synthetic oil refinery, approximately ten miles south of Leipzig, Germany.

As usual, Spleth and I spelled each other off flying formation until he took over for the bomb run at the IP. Up to that point, everything was routine.

On the bomb run, we saw the lead box picking up flak, but it wasn't much of a problem for us. Col. Rogner called on Command radio, and directed the Group not to release bombs because his bombardier had not been able to sight the target due to haze and smoke, and announced that we would return to the I. P. for a second run. Shortly thereafter he directed the deputy lead to take over for the second run, saying he had battle damage and an engine out, and was returning to base.

For our box, the second run was wild with deadly flak. Our box got separated from the lead box, and our box's lead bombardier took over bomb aiming for our box. We were caught by two very close bursts which did lot of damage. The No. 1 propeller ran away; I heard it going, it revved up like a bumblebee. In accordance with our crew SOP, I identified it with a glance at the tachs; I yanked the throttle away from Spleth and punched the feathering button--to no avail, it kept on buzzing. The No. 1 tach was indicating 3700 to 3900 rpm, and a severe left yaw developed. We didn't realize that Spleth's right rudder pedal was out of commission, so I wasn't helping with right rudder pedal correction .

Braffmann, down in the nose, called on the interphone, sounding pretty panicky, to ask if we pilots were O. K.

"I see an awful lot of red stuff running down here!"

We reassured him it must be hydraulic fluid, because we weren't hurt.

The No. 1 engine spun at its very high rpm quite smoothly for a while, but caused so much yaw and drag that we quickly dropped out of formation, unable to maintain position or keep up. Then it obviously ran out of oil and began to seize, causing severe vibration. The planetary reduction gears began chewing through the nose case, and the whole front of the engine glowed red from the heat of friction. The airplane shook more and more violently. I heard Cornell, back in the tail, banging against the sides of his compartment whenever he talked on interphone, and told him to get out of his position and come forward to the waist. I tried to call Briol, to tell him to get out of the ball turret, but the other gunners told me he was already out. Spleth alerted everybody to be prepared to bail out.

The engine gearing finally tore loose, leaving the now stopped crankshaft speared into the freely spinning hub of the flat pitched prop. The vibration died down, but the yaw and drag continued very high. We thought that if we could abruptly slow or yaw the airplane, the prop might pull itself off and spin away. But we didn't have electrical control of landing gear and flaps to help slow quickly, or enough variability of yaw control, to do it.

The tremendous drag caused us to burn a lot of extra gas

just to stay in the air, and we soon realized we'd never make it back to Glatton. We gradually traded some altitude for air speed, and fervently hoped we wouldn't encounter any fighters.

The G-box had caught fire and failed early in the mission. To that we had now added battle damage--No. 1 engine failed and prop windmilling, Spleth's right rudder pedal broken, brake hydraulic system out, wire bundles containing gear and flap control wiring cut, wiring to most (if not all) the radios out plus lots of holes. Grybos couldn't get out on the long range radio, either. We were surviving, but the bomber stream had long since disappeared, and Braffmann had only DR to navigate by, because we had a solid undercast. We kept asking him for refined headings, and to tell us when we were over friendly territory. After what seemed forever, he finally announced,

"We should be over Belgium--I think."
About that time, I spotted what appeared to be a hole in the undercast ahead and to the right. We went over and looked down. There was a beautiful runway, with P-47's parked on the field. As we circled down to approximate traffic pattern altitude, we tried calling on every frequency we knew. Command radio was definitely out, no answer.

Haynes started cranking furiously on the landing gear, finally getting indications that it was down and locked. By now, the ground folks were firing green flares from both ends of the runway. Spleth told everybody to take crash landing positions.

The landing was pretty good, but we soon found out we didn't have much directional control, and had no brakes at all. The airplane drifted off the runway to the left, aimed right at a "Follow Me" Jeep waiting to lead us to parking. I have never seen a Jeep go so fast.

Once off the hard surface into the soft grass, the airplane slowed abruptly, and the No. 1 prop fell off, jabbed one blade into the ground, and just stood there.

There was a row of 2 x 4's standing on end, parallel to the runway. Our drift continued across them, knocking several of them over, and the airplane came to a stop. After we cut the engines, the Jeep pulled up off the right wing, and the driver yelled over,

"That area past the 2 x 4's hasn't been cleared of land mines yet. Good luck!"

As we walked through the waist to leave, I noticed that the main entry door was missing.

"What happened to the door?" I asked.

"Oh, that," one of the gunners replied. "Back there when Spleth alerted us for bail out, we pulled the hinge pins. The door fell out when we landed."

We had landed at a forward base, near Mons, Belgium.

We went and looked at the prop. There was a flak hole in the prop dome about 3/4 inch across. No wonder it wouldn't feather!

We managed to get a message off to the 457th that evening, telling them where we were, and the condition of the airplane. (I'm not sure it got there.)

The P-47 outfit served much better meals than we usually get at Glatton; Swiss steak and fresh white bread, even.

By Lend-Lease arrangements, we stayed two nights in hotels in Mons. A Troop Carrier C-47, crew in fatigues, carried us to a base in France. There we switched to another C-47. The Air Transport Command crew on it was wearing Class A's. What a way to fight a war!

When we got back to the Base, we found out that all our gear had been impounded. Also, someone had taken a package I was saving to open at Christmas. I don't know what was in it.

The 748th Squadron Engineering Officer presented Spleth and me with a "Bill",

One (1) each B-17. . . . . $306,000

I almost forgot--while we were walking around on those cobblestones in Mons, the swelling in my right ankle went down, the bandaging is gone, and I can easily get my GI shoe on again.

Briol, Sunday, December 3, 1944

Went to Mass this morning, (Sunday). Our pass was cut down to two days. We're supposed to get it tonight. We were planning on going to Belfast, Ireland but now we can't go on such a short pass. Looks like this little fellow will spend his pass in Peterborough again.

A shower and shave surely felt good this morning after

being filthy for such a long time although the water was ice cold. We can't get paid because we were listed missing in action. The only thing I can do is get those francs changed again. The whole crew is broke.

After this pass we'll be flying a lot again because we're low on crews again after that last raid, no replacements coming in. If we'd been missing a few more hours they would have sent our folks that dreaded telegram that I never want them to get. We got back just in time. Over in Belgium there were alerts every half hour. Lot of flying bombs.

Briol, Tuesday, December 5, 1944

Got back from our pass today. That is, I'm back. The rest of the crew went to London. I spent all my time in Peterborough taking it easy, mostly. I've had enough excitement for a while.

Just got a letter from my "Mom" with a clipping saying I was promoted. It said, it was announced by Col. Luper. I can still see Col. Luper going down in flames over the target at Politz.

We have another worry now. The Germans are using their ME-163 ships to ram our planes. In other words, they just head their ship for us and crash into us.

Briol, Wednesday, December 6, 1944

Our crew didn't fly today. The rest of the squadron went to Merseburg again. I guess they're kind of giving us a rest. Zeiler's crew (the other crew in this hut) came back with three good engines, the other feathered. Wilson's crew isn't back from Belgium yet where they had to bail out, the same day we had to crash land there.

There was another man killed on the line this morning while they were putting their guns into the planes. Besides that, there were two men murdered outside the gate this week. I saw one of the men with the top of his head split open. At first they thought he had fallen off a bike and hit his head on a rock but it happened again and they figured it was murder.

It doesn't worry me. I figure it's easy to die with both feet on the ground, after going through what I have been in the air. We carry our .45's all the time now and believe me, I'm not afraid to kill any more.

There's been a lot of hijacking going on around here. I've found out that London is a dangerous place at night during the blackout. The time I went to London I was alone and when I got off at King's Cross, it was dark as pitch. I got directions to the Red Cross and started. Somebody was following me all right. I stepped into an alley and they went by. I think they were pretty tough characters. Our radio man had the same thing happen to him.

Storey, one of the crew who bailed out over Belgium just got back. He'll be telling us his experience. He had a more rough time of it than we had.

Our whole crew is trigger happy now. We shoot at the drop of a hat. I guess combat puts that instinct into us. I noticed it when I was partridge hunting with the English on our flak leave. Every time a bird flew up my gun was up there firing first. When it comes to shooting, I never hesitate anymore.

Briol , Thursday, December 7, 1944

We got up at three o'clock this morning and briefed for the bombing of Dortmund, Germany. We had our guns and equipment all in the plane when they scrubbed it. Zeiler's crew was still sleeping when we got back to the hut. We went back to the sack again about six thirty and slept peacefully till nine. Zeiler's crew wasn't on the loading list last night and neither were we but they put us on the last minute. We slept peacefully last night because we thought we wouldn't fly today.

I'm almost sorry they scrubbed the mission today because we haven't had such an easy one in a long time. I shouldn't say easy because no mission is easy, some are less rough than others.

We had to take some shots again today. My arm will probably be sore tomorrow. We have classes all day today. I saw in the Stars and Stripes where a gunner says he wants to go on missions because they're exciting. He's either a liar or he's crazy. It may sound exciting but when you see your buddies getting killed and you know you might be next, it's a dirty, filthy, bloody job. I know a fellow in another hut who would have put in his last mission, if we'd have flown today. He's the first in this squadron that ever came that close since I've been here. When I first got here, there were some who only had three or four to go before finishing, but they went down. I have about twelve missions to go yet before I can go home. Our tail gunner has thirteen to go. Spleth and Welch have about ten to go. The rest of our crew have the same as me, except our new waist gunner who has about twenty to go. His crew went down in flames over Germany. Our navigator has about three to go. His crew also went down in flames.

We just heard a British Lancaster in trouble overhead about an hour ago. We ran outside in time to see the whole crew of British airmen bailing out over our field here. They ran the ambulance out. A few of them were hurt. The plane went off over the horizon; we didn't see it crash. I don't know what the trouble was, yet.

These missions keep a guy dead tired all the time. They usually keep us pretty busy when we don't go on a raid, with classes, practice missions, etc. We usually have to work on our guns quite a bit. Our lives depend on them. When we get some spare time about the only thing we have energy for, is to fall into our bunks.

I should write more letters. We have to take them over and get them censored ourselves. Censor is busy, etc.

In one way I hope this will make up for it a little bit. I'll want Marcella to read this although it's a heck of a thing for a person to read. It isn't very cheerful. I've written all of this in a heck of a hurry. Sometimes I'll jot down a few lines when I come into the hut for my mess kit before I pull out for chow. Maybe it keeps me from going nuts. I have to get it out of my system some way.

Sometimes when the whole crew is together there'll be an incident that's bothering everybody. Someone will start it and then everybody will get it off their chests. It helps sometimes.

I really can't talk about much. I don't feel big about what we have to do over Germany. It makes me feel awfully low.

I surely look forward to Marcella's letters. I'd give a month's pay just to see that lovely little chick's face again. She's my little chick. Maybe that's not a nice expression for me to make. I don't think she'd mind, though.

Briol, Friday, December 8, 1944 ^

There was a stand down all night last night, so there was no raid today. We had classes this morning. There'll be classes this afternoon and a practice mission. These classes are mighty boring. S-2 lectures, intelligence lectures, P. O. W. lectures, VD lectures, etc. We're supposed to check and clean our guns, too.

Welch, December 8, 1944

In spite of rough times, the pressure has eased in the last month. The group flew eleven missions in November, our crew only five. Weather has cut the flying rate, and new crews have been arriving. Some of them trained in B-24's, have never been in B-17's. They'll learn fast. The new crew manning goal is 25 crews per squadron, so we shouldn't have to fly more than half the missions.

Right after we got back from flak shack, the Ops. Officer said he'd like to make us a lead crew, and asked how many missions we had. Spleth told him he had 20, and the rest of the crew one or two less. The Ops. Officer said that was too many, and we would just go ahead and fly most of our missions in the slot, leading the low element. That's where we've been for most of our missions.

Once in a while when we're not flying a mission I'll take one of the new pilots who has only B-24 4-engine experience, and anyone else we can round up, and we go out and fly a little for practice, looking over the country side, practicing landings, etc. A few days ago we were out, and chased a Stirling until we were in formation with him. We were a bit humbled when we could barely keep up with him and then noticed that he had one feathered.

Things have sure changed since 3 years ago yesterday.

Briol, Mission No. 24, Saturday, December 9, 1944
Group Mission No. 157

Today we bombed a German airfield at Stuttgart, Germany. Our group didn't have any losses.

We saw the group in front of us being attacked by

German jet propulsion planes. I've never seen anything so fast in all my life. There were only a few of them. They made one pass before our fighters were after them. I recognized them by the smoke rings behind them. Our fighters got some of them but they easily outran our fighters.

I saw a couple fighters falling and I saw two of our Fortresses in that group go down in flames. One Fortress just spun all the way down with a long column of black smoke behind it. No one got out of it. The other Fortress broke into three parts, burning. One wing came off and the fuselage broke right in half at the radio room. I don't think anyone lived in that one either.

We weren't touched by flak today. There was some after we got over the enemy lines and there was quite a bit over Stuttgart and some over the target but we evaded most of it. We carried about 40 bombs, each weighing about 100 lbs. These bombs are used mostly for killing humans. We killed plenty.

I flew the nose today as a toggalier for the first time in combat. I threw the switch that dropped the bombs out of the bomb bay. Ozzie usually flies that position. The toggalier also mans the Chin Turret guns.

Our gas load today was 2,780 gallons. The temperature up there was 65 degrees below zero Centigrade, which also would be about 85 degrees below zero Fahrenheit. I can't describe that intense cold.

It was a long, long trip to southern Germany. We formed over the Glatton low frequency Buncher in England, then flew south, way down to the southern tip of England. We passed over London on the way. Then we flew over the Channel into France, into Germany.

We also flew over Paris. Everywhere you looked in France you saw bomb craters. We came back the same way but we had to leave the formation to descend because we started to run out of oxygen.

This morning when we started engines on the ground, No. 3 caught fire and ruined it, so we couldn't use it. We used the spare ship and it was low on Oxygen. Besides that, over the target our oxygen system sprang a leak. We stayed up there as long as we could but we were getting kind of woozy. We were getting enough oxygen to live, but it was causing harm. Soon as we got into friendly territory we descended to a safer and warmer altitude. We could relax then, a little. We all felt terrible as usual, after straining our eyes all day to the utmost, on the alert for fighters and flak, tense and scared, the intense cold and the weakness of one's body at high altitude. A few minutes at high altitude like that saps much more energy than working for hours on the ground.

After I relaxed, I had a terrific headache, probably from lack of oxygen. I almost went completely blind for about ten minutes. I didn't know if it was from straining my eyes in the sunlight or what.

I didn't care much. After a guy goes through this much he doesn't care what happens. I didn't say anything but I closed my eyes for a while and it cleared away. We beat the rest of the group back this time.

After I got my shot of whiskey, it braced me up a great deal. I'm in my sack right now and I can't keep my eyes open. My bones and muscles ache all over. I'm getting awfully old. Most of my crew is asleep already. I know now that I have pilot's fatigue.

I still receive absolution and Communion before each mission, and no matter what time we come over to the chapel, Father Ludder is there, waiting for us. Sometimes it's midnight and cold, or it's one or two or three in the morning. I'll be a God fearing man as long as I live.

These mornings the mud on this base is always frozen solid and there is lots of mud.

We had one full meal today. That was late tonight and I didn't even feel much like eating. This is no lie: just before we landed I was so tired I was testing myself by thinking of my crew members' names. I actually couldn't remember them. For five minutes I couldn't think of Cornell's name or Grybos, Haynes, Ozzie, Karl or hardly even my own. I'm quite a sad sack.

Spleth, Mission No. 26, Group Mission No. 157,
December 9, 1944 (Saturday), #4 high (796)
Target: Sindelfingen, Germany (Near Stuttgart)

Take off and assembly O. K.. Weather over target bad, but we climbed to 30,000 to get over it.

We were low on oxygen, having just enough to get off

the bomb run. Had to leave formation before getting out of enemy territory and get down so as to be able to breathe some good old air again.

Returned just ahead of the formation, was met by the Major as he thought we had aborted.

No flak at target. Turned sharp to right to keep out of Stuttgart flak.

Briol, Sunday, December 10,1944

The raid for today (Sunday) was scrubbed early this morning about one o'clock. Rain and fog set in. It's so foggy now, you can't see a block. There's a cold light rain coming down. Everything is muddy.

I went to Mass this morning over in our little theater on the base.

Although we haven't got our original ship anymore, the name of our plane is "Fireball Special". It's after our squadron insignia. Our own ship is still being repaired in sub depot. The ship we crashed and left in Belgium was not ours. You can't expect to keep a Fortress whole with everyone shooting at you all the time. The ship we have now, I don't think will ever be repaired. They should condemn it. We should have named it "Old Ironsides".

I don't know what's cooking. They're equipping a lot of the Fortresses with bomb bay tanks. I'm afraid it means long, long trips of some kind.

Briol, Monday, December 11, 1944

Our target for today was Frankfurt. Our crew didn't complete the mission because we flew spare. Each crew gets that a couple times during their tour. We flew as far as the coast of France, turned around and came back. The spares always go along with the formation to the coast. If one of the ships has to fall out, the spare fills in for him.

Both ways, we flew over London and on the coast, the White Cliffs of Dover. We flew very low over the Cliffs of Dover. We got back about one o'clock this afternoon. The rest of the group today messed things up and missed the target. Before we turned back, we were directly over Calais, France.

147

We're taking precautions again against strafing Germans. It's been happening again. Every Fortress we have sitting on the field has its Top Turret guns installed and ready to fire all the time. There would be a lot of lead flying if every top turret in every ship on the field was firing.

Briol, Mission No. 25, Tuesday, December 12, 1944
Group Mission No. 159

We were over Germany today almost the same time the sun came up. We saw the sun rise and set on Germany. Our primary target for today was Lutzkendorf. The secondary if it was PFF was to be Merseburg. We ended up by bombing Merseburg. We carried twelve 500 lb. bombs. Our gas load was 2,700 gallons, a long trip. We went over the Channel, Belgium and far into Germany.

The crew and I get more scared and jumpy on every mission. We practically snap at anyone who gets in our way now.

We came through with hardly a hole again. We saw no enemy fighters, but there was plenty of flak. Right after bombs away, the flak was getting our range and creeping up on us. I was so jumpy, I couldn't help hollering over the interphone, "Bank to the right, bank to the right, look out for that flak at nine o'clock!" We moved over and it went blasting away beside us.

Our box was scattered all over today. The last six ships were straggling. It wasn't quite so cold today, 39 degrees below zero. At least it wasn't cold compared to the other one of 65 degrees below zero Centigrade. On the way back we saw some German rocket bombs headed for Belgium and England.

On the bomb run we had a terrific tail wind at altitude which gave us a ground speed of almost 400 miles per hour but going back we had to fight that wind and it slowed us down almost to 120 miles an hour. It seemed like we'd never get out of Germany.

The sun had almost set by the time we got to Belgium. It was dark when we got to England and there was a heavy fog again. We narrowly missed hitting other ships again as we came in. About all we could see was the runway lit up with its orange lights. They shot up flares to show us where the end of the runway was. We found the field by radio compass. We wouldn't get very far without these navigation aids and when they get shot out, it puts us on a spot.

Zeiler's crew got shot up quite a bit but we're still all together in this little hut.

The Germans were blasting at us with red, white, black and yellow flak. Some of it, I can't figure out. That shot of whiskey put me on my feet again after landing. Gosh, how I hate to get up these cold mornings, sometimes at midnight, especially to go out and get shot at. I know it won't last forever, though, so I still have a lot to look forward to if things go right.

Spleth, Mission No. 27, Group Mission No. 159
December 12, 1944 (Tuesday), Lead high-high (606)
Target: Merseburg, Germany

Plenty dark when we took off, also soupy. Climbed through the overcast and assembled.

Went over target and our box got no flak. Came back O. K. but was really sweating out gasoline. However we had plenty. Had camera so we left formation early and came in. Poor visibility landing. No battle damage.

Welch, Mission No. 26, Group Mission No. 159
Tuesday, December 12, 1944

We flew about nine hours today. Only about four missions have been longer. It was dark for take off and for landing.

The sun was getting pretty low as we crossed Belgium in our bomber stream on return. Ahead of us and below, we saw specks appear in the sky. They turned into Lancasters and Stirlings as they got closer, looking for all the world like a swarm of bees, down at about 18,000 feet. The RAF was going out on a night bombing raid somewhere, (maybe many wheres) in Germany. Here and there two or three ships were in a formation of sorts. I guess that was just buddies flying along together for the fun of it. We understand that basically each crew navigates on its own, and either bombs on its own or on fires started by "Pathfinder". They don't believe in high altitude, daylight bombing in formation.

Figure 15. Eighth Air Force Insignia

CHAPTER XI

THE WEATHER TURNS WORSE

Briol, Wednesday, December 13, 1944

We didn't fly today. It's cold and foggy out. We had a bunch of lectures and discussions.

The alert just sounded. We're expecting some air attacks from the Germans. No one seems very worried about it.

Nothing happened, the all clear sounded.

We've been having wonderful fighter support lately. It makes us feel much more secure on our missions. It's really different from when I first started flying here.

The fighters never have to go through flak like we do (the bombers). They can stay away from the flak areas or dodge them. We have to keep plodding on and on right through them most of the time. At the target we just can't evade much flak because we have to try to fly straight and level to hit the target. The fighters can just "set" out around the target and watch the bombers head straight into those thousands of black puffs. Just one black puff will blow up a whole Fortress. I have seen fighters go down from flak, though, too. Another thing about a fighter, they have only one engine and if that engine goes out, they're done for, unless it's a twin engine fighter.

The Germans are increasing their flak guns all the time. They have more flak over Leipzig, now, than they have over Berlin. Over fifty bombers were lost the last time we went to Leipzig. That's the time we had to crash in Belgium.

I've never seen such a heavy fog in England yet, as we have today. We can't see more than thirty feet in any direction. It's cold to boot.

We got in some more new crews today to replace our losses. These new crews are always so eager. We old crews have all the eagerness knocked out of us, in more ways than one.

Briol, Saturday, December 16, 1944

Our crew got a 48 hour pass. Most of us got back a

little while ago. I spent my pass in Peterborough again. Took in a couple dances and visited a few pubs. It's still foggy as the dickens and it was raining a little for a while. It's quite cold, too, but there's no snow. The last time we were in Germany, the ground was covered with snow.

We've been living in mud almost ever since we got here. Sometimes we sleep with our clothes on to keep warm. The rats don't bother us any more. Guess they don't like our company. I'll say this much, our chow is nothing to brag about, but it's much better than the meals we buy in town here in England

Briol, Sunday, December 17, 1944

It's still foggy and wet, so there's still no flying. I went to Mass this morning, (Sunday). Met a fellow today whose crew I knew at Drew Field, Florida. His was a hard luck crew. He's the only one alive on it now. They were from another field close by. Something went wrong every time they flew. Their radio gunner was killed by flak on about the tenth mission. The pilot was wounded by flak on the next mission. He wouldn't quit flying, though. When he got out they aborted on the next mission and the spare flew in their place. The spare went down. On the Merseburg raid their ship exploded over the target. No one had a chance. This guy is still here because he didn't fly with his crew that day.

We had a good sermon at Mass today. Father Ludder writes a letter to the folks of every Catholic that dies in combat from this base. He says it's pretty tough to write sometimes because they don't always receive the sacraments before taking off.

I couldn't sleep last night. I lay in my bunk smoking a cigarette and listening to the rain and the wind and just thinking. I was thinking of thousands of horrible things that could happen to me over enemy territory. Home, Marcella, what my next raid had in store for me. It's the same uncertainty every day..

Briol, Monday, December 18, 1944

Thirteen of our ships flew today but our crew didn't . It seems like none of the old crews flew today.

We're listening to Germany over the radio right now, I

like their music better than the English music. When this group (457th) first came to England the Germans welcomed them over the radio. It was a German woman. She told them exactly what time they arrived, how strong they were, and she said they were looking forward to a visit from our bombers soon. To top it off she told them to look at the clock in the 457th operations office, that it was five minutes slow. They looked and sure enough she was right.

I ran into a friend today who looked like he saw a ghost when he saw me. He said he had seen the missing in action list. Naturally we were on it when we landed in Belgium. He didn't think we were still alive.

Early this morning there was a tremendous explosion a short distance from here--a German buzz bomb. They rarely come down this far. An alert woke us up but we just went back to sleep again. We woke up again when the explosion almost threw us out of bed.

Our ships came back late this afternoon. They didn't get to the target. The target was to be Cologne.

Briol, Tuesday, December 19, 1944

Our crew still didn't go on a raid today. They flew most of the new crews again. We were down there to watch them come back. One ship completely nosed over and caught fire. They hit pretty hard. Most of them were dead. We jumped on a truck going out there. They had all the bodies out when we got there. Burning flesh is the most sickening smell a man would want to experience. I wish I'd have gone back to my hut instead. This is the way things work around here.

When an accident occurs because of frost bite or lack of oxygen, there's a big fuss made about it. We get lectures and everything else on it but when the enemy hits us and we lose a lot of men, well, that's war, it was a line of duty. Not much is said about it, except to have your guns in better order and things like that.

Someone flew our ship, (Fireball Special). Now "Fireball Special." is no more. Need I say more? We have another ship now and our name is "Dead Engine Kids". We figured it was a good name because we've come in so often with engines dead and shot away.

It's usually customary when a different crew goes down and it's not their ship, the original crew names their next ship the same name, only they put a number after it, such as two, three, etc. It usually happens, though, that the plane and the crew it belongs to, both go down.

It's foggy as the dickens out again. It's a little warmer, though.

I'm afraid I've lost my good naturedness. I wanted to fight with a guy before, just because he said something I didn't like. I feel pretty silly over it now.

Briol, Wednesday, December 20, 1944

There was no mission again today. A lot of ships got off the ground and had to land at another base. They couldn't land here again. I've never seen such a fog. It's a cold fog, too, and goes right through a person. I doubt if there'll be a mission for some time. It's giving us quite a rest although we have classes all the time to occupy us. I'd sooner get the rest of these missions over with. It's not easy to sit around and wonder what's in store for you.

We saw a movie today on what not to do when flying. It reminded me of cadet days, when I used to go up alone in a Stearman 220 horsepower biplane. I remember I dove over a house three times one day in Florida. I buzzed a guy in a cornfield. I flew right off the roof of a school bus, practically. Once, the temptation was too great. I dragged my landing gear through a treetop waving at a girl. I buzzed a guy in a boat and he almost fell in the water.

Welch, December 20, 1944

The weather has been so bad that the number of missions has drastically declined, and our crew hasn't flown for over a week. Over on the Continent the German Army has taken advantage of the miserable weather and heavy cloud cover to counter attack in the Belgium and Luxemburg area. We'd desperately like to go and help our guys, but it's so stinko here as well as there that we can't even get off the ground.

We have a laughable situation here, except that it's hard to laugh when you're cold. About last September a huge pile of coke was delivered to the base, to be used for heating for the winter. A man from each hut would go and get enough to keep the hut's stove going, each day. About a month ago, the Supply people noticed that with only about a fourth of the heating season gone, only about a third of the winter's supply of coke was left. So they put a fence around it, and began rationing it, a shovelful for each hut each day, and if there isn't a man at the hut to receive it when they come around to deliver it, that hut doesn't get any that day.

Some of the guys have rigged up systems to burn used airplane engine oil. That's kind of risky because a lot of it has been diluted with aviation gasoline. You could get an explosion, or a bigger fire than bargained for.

For a while, there was an alternative. When the base was built, they had to cut down a bunch of trees. They were still lying around. So some of the guys checked axes and saws out of Supply, and cut the logs up into firewood. When all the logs inside the fence were used up, they started cutting up those lying outside the fence. A day came when they were all gone, too. So one fine (?) day, someone cut a tree down. There was quite an uproar, because all trees in England belong to the King, and it requires very special permission to cut one down. So there went that source of heat. Our coke is enough to heat the hut for about two hours in the evening, except on the days when we're all out flying a mission and no one is here to receive our shovelful of coke. We spend a lot more time at the club, which somehow gets coke.

Karl Lambertson has been flying as a full time replacement for John Byknish, whom the Flight Surgeon grounded. John lost two stripes--he's now a Corporal--and has been put in charge of the Skeet Range. He's just about the happiest man on the base.

Briol, Thursday, December 21, 1944

No flying. Had to attend classes and combat movies, most of the day. They show us air battles and tactics of the enemy. They show us planes battling it out and going down in flames. I wouldn't mind watching that stuff but we know we have to go out and <u>really</u> see it again soon. They pull no punches in these films and lectures. They show men getting

155

blasted to pieces and everything else, as if we haven't seen enough.

It's still foggy, muddy and cold out. We have to practically swim to chow in mud and water. We had another alert. The bomb struck a long ways off, though.

Ozzie was pretty sick. The tail gunner on Zeiler's crew is sick today. The Ball Turret gunner on Zeiler's crew had to have an operation. I'm holding up very well but I'm always very tired and scared.

I have that dazed feeling all the time. I've got so I hate all antiaircraft gunners. Yes, even our own. I detest anyone with both his feet on solid ground while we're up there suffering from a thousand things and flying helplessly through their intense barrages, knowing any second we may be blasted to bits or die a slow death in agony. I'm glad sometimes when some of our bombs go wild and hit those flak towers and blast those crews to bits.

We have to kill or be killed when enemy fighter planes hit us, too, but we feel different towards them. They have the same problems as we have.

It takes a very powerful gun and a very large, heavy projectile to reach us from the ground. You may as well say they're cannons.

There are a lot of fellows who refuse to fly after a mission or two. It usually doesn't go easy with them.

I'd wish we'd get these missions done. It gives me too much time to think this way. When I feel pretty low, I take Marcella's picture out and look at it and then I feel like I'm not doing this for nothing. I'm certainly a long ways from feeling like a hero, though. I want to live as much as the next guy. I'd sooner be a live coward than a dead hero any day. I don't know what I'm kicking about. Look at those poor infantry guys, too. They deserve the credit also.

Briol, Friday, December 22, 1944

It's still foggy and wet out. We had some classes today; otherwise we took it pretty easy. Our ground forces are falling back in Belgium and we can't do a thing to help yet. It would be suicide to fly in this weather. Christmas carols on the radio. What torture, I can't enjoy them.

Briol, Friday, December 23, 1944

No flying. Still foggy. We shot skeet all morning to keep in practice. I've always got the highest score on skeet but today Ozzie beat me. He had eighteen and I had seventeen. This afternoon we have classes all afternoon. Bomb results, other theaters and other tactics. I don't like other theaters. It suggests we may have to go to the China, India, Burma Theater. I've seen enough of this war without going over there.

Welch, December 24-25, 1944

This has been a day. We briefed early this morning for a maximum effort mission to bomb Coblenz, in support of our ground troops west of there. The idea was to disrupt the German supply lines. The maximum effort meant four boxes of 12 ships each. I was assigned to fly as first pilot with a new crew on its first mission. The fog was pretty thick, I had trouble seeing the airplane taxiing ahead of us.

We were taking off on Runway 6. There are railroad tracks across the departure path just past the end of the runway. The first six airplanes got off all right, but the seventh got his wing down crossing the railroad tracks, and it caught a railway wagon (small freight car) and crashed in the field beyond. By order of Col. Rogner, take offs were halted while the crash crew and the fire department tried to find the crashed airplane. After we'd sat there stirring up the fog for quite a while, take offs were further delayed, and we taxied back to our hardstand, where we shut down our engines. Almost everybody went to chow.

About one o'clock, crews were ordered back to their airplanes, this time for only three boxes, so the new crew and I were stood down. The ships that went got off around two o'clock. After about two or two and a half hours, we could hear them overhead, but the fog was so thick nobody could land, so they were diverted to some other base with hopefully better weather.

Midnight Mass wasn't nearly as well attended as Father Ludder had expected, and a lot of the choir was absent. With a lot of the planned-for diners absent, those of us there had a surplus of goodies for our Christmas dinner.

We didn't get back to the base till tonight. What a red hot miserable Christmas we had. First of all on the night of December 23, we didn't get much sleep. There was a drunken party going on in camp. Men brought women from town down here to their huts.

England is full of filth. You get so you detest everything around here. They were out shooting their pistols into the air and we were expecting a couple slugs through the hut any second. About three o'clock the next morning, (December 24) the red alert woke us up. I couldn't believe my ears. The Germans were actually overhead and we were waiting for the bombs to hit. We heard the ack ack gunners go into action. The bombs hit not far from here. There was plenty concussion. Our ack ack gunners blazed away for about fifteen minutes.

A half hour later we were told we'd brief for a mission. It was still foggy. I didn't see how we'd get off. We were to hit an airfield right next to Koblenz, Germany. The fog was mighty thick but we had to take off. Sundbaum's crew was in front of us and they met disaster. As they started down the runway, the ship swerved from side to side going too fast to stop. It left the runway, smashed through a parked truck and went through the fence. It was about a yard off the ground now. The left wing dipped down just as it came to the train on the railroad tracks. The wing hit the train and lifted one of the huge freight cars right off the track and smashed it to the ground. The wing was also sheared off. The rest of the plane came down and crashed right next to an English farm house and started to burn. I can't understand why the bombs didn't explode right away. Four men were killed instantly. The rest of the men staggered out and got away from the plane, some on their hands and knees. They were all injured. The fire got to the bombs and they exploded. It took about half the farm house away, too. I think there were some dead in the house. They found nothing left of the bodies left in the plane.

Our takeoff was delayed then. I was listening over command radio and I never heard so much cursing and swearing over a radio. Everyone wanted a scrub because it was suicide to take off in this stuff. Everybody was nervous, it was a bad start. This was to be a record day for the 8th Air Force, so we took off. (Ed.: About 2 p. m.)

We got back to England and got to our base to find it all fogged over. We were diverted to another field. It was dark now. We flew northeast until we came to the coast again. There, we narrowly missed crashing coming in, in the dark. There was confusion all over. We went around again and missed the treetops by inches. I felt the plane slip and braced for the crash but we made it.

We had landed at the base named "Eye" in the Third Division. This was our Christmas Eve. Our whole group landed there, so there was really no room. We had to sleep on a cement floor while we were there. We were also supposed to fly another mission on Christmas. They were going to overhaul and load the ship. Thank goodness that base was fogged in so no one could take off. We had corned beef and cabbage for Christmas dinner. We had turkey for supper anyway and it was mighty good. Our plans for Midnight Mass and church were spoiled. We were all stiff from sleeping on the floor. We were dirty and miserable. Very poor facilities for cleaning up.

We waited around in the cold and fog for the fog to lift, we wanted to get back. It didn't lift so we slept on the floor again. This morning, (December 26) we got up early but had to wait till afternoon before we took off. We got back here late this afternoon. Parts of Sundbaum's ship were still laying beside the shattered building as we flew in for a landing.

We have two new crew men in this hut who have not flown a mission yet and are scared. They hear us talking, they heard that plane blow up that day. It's not good.

Spleth, Mission No. 28, Group Mission No. 162
December 24, 1944 (Sunday), #4 lead box (591 W)
Target: Originally Coblenz, Germany, actually 40 miles
out in the Channel.

Went to early morning briefing, but could not take off on account of weather. Most of one box got off--one ship cracked up on take off. We stood by till 1400, and took off in the soup. Assembled and headed for the Channel at 10,000 ft. Dropped bombs in Channel 40 miles out, and returned to base but could not land. Was diverted to 490th Group. Stayed there that night and Christmas Day (Ate a good turkey dinner that night), and took off about noon Dec. 26. Poor visibility . All O. K.

Briol, Mission No. 27, Group Mission No. 163, Wednesday, December 27, 1944

Our target for today was Gerolstein, Germany, quite close to Koblenz. We bombed the marshalling yards. We were awakened at two o'clock this morning. We went down to the orderly room, got our pass to briefing, received Communion and went to breakfast. After briefing we worked on our guns and the ship as usual before we took off.

It was still foggy when we took off but no matter what happens, we're always back for more punishment, we're crazy. Our route was over the Channel, Belgium, into Germany. We were supposed to expect enemy fighters again but we didn't see any this time. There was flak bursting at us all the time we were in Germany. It wasn't too heavy over the target although it was quite accurate. I didn't see any planes go down but it left a lot with shot engines and they straggled. Some didn't get back, so I don't know. We got to the target and the high box dropped their bombs. They hit all over in the buildings and everything else except the marshalling yards. What a messed up deal.

Before we dropped ours, the other two boxes were ordered to make a 360 and go over it again. The second time around, I watched the bombs come tearing across the marshalling yards blowing everything sky high. There was one little village down there that was wiped right off the earth.

On the way out we were dodging flak right and left. We had only one little hole in our right wing.

I can't explain how a guy feels on a bomb run. He's always waiting for that one explosion that will put him into oblivion. As you get closer to the target your heart beats faster and faster. You breathe harder and harder but there's no air to breathe. Even when it's 50 below you forget about the cold. Your nerves are strung up almost to the breaking point. You can feel every blood vessel in your body bulging. You're so nervous and scared that every time there's a burst of flak or the plane jumps a little, you think, "This is the end". I used to do it without flinching but now I'm liable to do anything. Still we go back for more. I can't say much. When we got back to the field it was still partly foggy but we touched sweet Mother Earth once more.

Spleth, Mission No. 29, Group Mission No. 163,
December 27, 1944 (Wednesday) #4 high box (591 W)
Target: Gerolstein, Germany, Railroad Bridge

Early briefing, including two blankets and K-rations for two days. I took off and changed seats with Welch. Short mission, lots of uncharted flak. Made 360 over target. Believed to be good mission. I also landed as there was poor visibility. Came back to base instead of landing on continent. No battle damage.

Briol, Thursday, December 28, 1944

Our Group didn't fly today. It's quite clear out, though, and it's warming up a little. The new crews are up on a practice mission. I just came back from chow, they had beans. Just saw a bunch of tanks go by out on the road.

I think we helped things yesterday. We went for transportation and communication facilities. Just about every group had their own target yesterday. We were in an area of hills where railroads criss-crossed everywhere. We flew over many targets that were already smoking and burning. Germany was covered with snow. When we were over England and looked down, the trees looked like snow balls. Everything was white from the previous fog which was frozen and covered every thing.

Major Glen Miller is still missing. The Nazi guns know no rank. When they shoot us down and we're armed to the teeth, I can imagine what happened to an unarmed ship.

Briol, Friday, December 29, 1944

Us old crews didn't fly today but the rest of the group did. This morning we had gunnery training. We split some wood for our stove in between times. We'll probably have films and lectures this afternoon. The weather is very nice today, just a little hazy. Our engineer and radio man had to get up early to test flight a ship.

The Germans are not advancing now. It helps to get the Air Force back into action. I'm not claiming any credit though. I don't know if I wrote this down but our first mission was flown in late August or early September. We have only a few missions to go. I'm sweating them out intensely. There were a few missions that we didn't get credit for.

It's true we're not over here as long as a lot of ground troops but during that time we see much more action than a lot of ground troops. We don't do as much ground slogging but the misery of high altitude makes up for it. It's such a beautiful day out today that it's hard to imagine that we'll be in terror over Nazi skies again soon.

Briol, Saturday, December 30, 1944

Our crew didn't fly again. Zeiler's crew flew. We'll be down to the line to sweat them in tonight. We have classes right now. Went to a dance last night at the Aero Club.

Briol, Mission No. 28, Group Mission No. 166, Sunday, December 31, 1944

Our target for today was Krefeld. (Sunday) The day before New Year. There was more to that name but I forgot it. Our gas load was 2,500 gallons. Our bomb load was over twenty 250 lb. bombs.

I saw no casualties today, except one. It was a sickening one. It happened over Holland, one of the Fortresses caught fire. There was no flak near them. In fact there was no flak near to any of us at that spot. One man bailed out of the waist door. The second man to come out was sucked right into the propeller of the Fortress flying a little below and behind them. All you could see was little bits that looked like clothing going back with the slipstream.

All the rest of the men did all right. Two pulled the rip cords right away and were left dangling from their parachutes at altitude. Even if they passed out, I think they dropped fast enough to come to, when they hit low altitude.

162

At the target there was a lot of flak. It came close but we didn't get hit. Our right wing man got hit and fell back. I don't know what happened to him. Some of the ships got holes. All our bombs left the ship, except five. We salvoed them. We blasted the marshalling yards sky high. I watched the bombs exploding as wave after wave of bombers went over.

We finally got out of the flak and headed back over Belgium for England once more. I was too tired to take part in it but there was a New Year's party at the Aero Club tonight. It was a drunken brawl, fights galore.

Spleth, Mission No. 30, Group Mission No. 166,
December 31 (Sunday), #4 high box (591 W)
Target: Krefeld, Germany

We were a little doubtful about the outcome of this mission when we were briefed. They said there were 240 guns on the target.

Take off was in the dark. Old W worked fine, and I wore a different heated suit that worked swell. Everything was S. O. P. and we got to the target to find very little flak and no fighter opposition.

We had poor results, dropping our bombs way left of the target. No trouble landing and no battle damage.

Easy mission. Five bombs would not go out in train and had to be salvoed.

Welch, New Year's Eve

There was kind of a noisy party at the Officers' Club this evening. I had a gin and orange, and watched. One first pilot who should have made First Lieutenant when Spleth did is still a Second Lieutenant, although his copilot and I have been First Lieutenants for a while. He has drilled holes in a set of gold bars and put bronze Oak Leaf Clusters on them. (There has been an administrative goof some where.) He kept coming up behind Col. Rogner and polishing his Eagles with a clean white handkerchief, and directing the Colonel's attention to his OLC gold bars. Whether it does any good, Col. Rogner certainly should be aware of the situation, now.

As the evening wore on, the party got rowdier. Things

kind of came to a head when a First Lieutenant jumped in Col. Rogner's Jeep and drove off at a high rate of speed. The MP's found the Jeep later, still on base. And we found out later that the "borrower" was none other than our crew's own Ted Braffmann. We don't think he'll get any worse than a reprimand.

It's a good thing there's no mission tomorrow. If this Group is typical, we'd look like the RAF going out on a mission.

CHAPTER XII

HAPPY NEW YEAR?

Briol, New Year's Day, 1945

Our crew didn't fly today but the rest of the Group did. I think they're flying a mighty tough mission today. I'll know later. Some other crew is flying our ship. In yesterday's raid the Luftwaffe was up after us. We didn't know it or see them. They shot down thirty-eight bombers from some other groups. There were fifty-two enemy planes shot down. The bombers accounted for twenty-six of them. Mighty, mighty good for those bombers. They were really on the ball. There was plenty shooting going on at the base here last night.

Our Fortresses came back about an hour ago. They were all the way over to the other side of Germany, almost to Poland, in the Berlin area. The high box came close to being attacked by enemy fighters. The escort fought them off. Most of the bombs today were delayed action. They hit the ground and bury themselves, or they embed themselves in a building. Hours later they explode. They are the booby trap type, too. If anyone tampers with them, they explode immediately. They were huge 1,000 lb. bombs, too. Some explode on impact. When the Germans start cleaning up, it's oblivion for them.

I heard explosions here in England all afternoon today, I know what it was now. Believe it or not, there were about 20 enemy fighters over England today strafing and bombing our airfields. I was actually shocked. Our fighters shot down about four planes. The British antiaircraft gunners shot down one. Fifteen of those enemy planes got away safely. I was surprised. I thought those explosions were practice.

We're expecting more attacks tonight. They haven't hit our base for a long time. We have very few air raid shelters here.

Briol, Mission No. 29, Group Mission No. 168,
Tuesday, January 2, 1945

Our target for today was Mayen, quite close to Frankfurt,

Germany. The German Luftwaffe was up today again. I watched a horrible but glorious air battle between their fighters and ours. They tried to penetrate through to the bombers but they didn't make it. I watched them fighting it out just over a cloud base. Many Germans went to their death. The 20 mm's from the German fighters looked like flak, over the cloud base. When I heard the report "Bandits" in the area, I jumped like I was shot.

Our group was the first over the target. We were missing two bombers from our box of twelve when we returned. There has been no report.

Before we got to the target we came close to being blasted to bits by flak. It was very accurate. I had my turret turned forward and all of a sudden there were five tremendous explosions right in front of our nose. None of the fragments hit us. It was another miracle! They were tracking us all the way to the target and back but the rest wasn't quite so accurate.

We bombed the marshalling yards of this town. The railroads went right through the center of the town. "Bombs away," and Ozzie hit the toggle switch. A while later the bombs hit. This was a little city of about 2,000 people. We blasted the yards all right and the entire city with it. The whole city was blasted to bits. There wasn't a square foot that wasn't touched. I saw the whole city disappearing and I suddenly realized again what a rotten business this was. There were Catholics down there and probably a lot of innocent people. There are still people in Germany who will help American airmen too. We were told in briefing if we were knocked down in Germany and lived we should try to get in touch with Catholic Germans.

If we fall into most German hands now, they will kill us. The Germans are making one last stand, on the ground and in the air. They're doing a good job of it too, I have to say.

McCall's crew went down. They've been down three days now and we only found out today. They were our best friends at Langley Field. They sweated us out when we crashed in Belgium. They were about the only ones who were really glad to see us back, and now . . . . .

I just heard the news. They said over half of the force of enemy fighters who were up after us today, were shot down. There must have been 130 shot down. It's getting plenty dangerous but our fighters are doing a good job of getting the enemy before they get to us, so we can fulfill our mission and get to the target. When I first started here it was a bit different.

I'm so tired I just can't do a thing. I haven't very many missions to put in now before going home. No one will ever know how I dread these last missions. I'm sweating them out and I get more high strung on each one, like tightening up a string on a violin and waiting for it to break. I feel so funny now, I couldn't go back and read all this stuff I've written. The only thing to do is forget it. I should write a letter but I can't even think straight now.

Spleth, Mission 31, Group Mission No. 168, January 2, 1945 (Tuesday) #1 High element, High squadron, Group was Division Lead; Target: Mayen, Germany

Took off and assembled in the dark--both S. O. P. Long bomb run in to the target--ground speed 145. Very few bursts of flak. Bombs away O. K., good pattern, hit over a little.

Did a lot of S-ing on way back. Ships kept dropping out till only 3 were left. Visibility poor when landing. No battle damage. Easy mission.

Briol, Wednesday, January 3, 1945, Group Mission No. 169

No flying for our crew today although we were on the loading list last night. The rest of the group is flying. Zeiler's crew, the other crew in this hut, are flying. They woke them up about three o'clock this morning. I instinctively wake up every time the C. Q. comes in. When he said we weren't flying, I practically fell apart, I relaxed so much.

We've been on our way to Germany long before the sun comes up lately. On our last mission it was a bit hazy but when we gained altitude over England the moon was almost overhead shining down on the haze below. About an hour later the east started lighting up and it was light up high long before it got light on the ground. There's something deathly about watching the lead ships in the dark shooting out their different colored flares, calling their broods together.

We're scheduled for the usual classes and lectures again for today.

A buzz bomb exploded on the field here late this afternoon. Both crews were in the hut when the alert sounded. As usual we didn't pay too much attention to it, until we heard that motor cycle sound. We rushed outside to see it almost overhead. When that engine quits you know it's coming down. Its nose went down and it started its steep glide. That's all we needed. There were no air raid shelters right here. The whole two crews of us dived right into the ditch of muddy water. Never even felt the mud as we lay in it face down hugging the ground. There was quite a concussion but it didn't hit too close to us.

Our group bombed Cologne today. It wasn't too tough a mission. I wish I'd have gone, too. No enemy fighters and very little flak.

Briol, Thursday, January 4, 1945

There was a stand down all last night. This field didn't fly today. We had a gunner's critique this morning. We'll have classes this afternoon. The new crews are up on a practice mission. I can hear the roar of our group overhead now.

Briol, Friday, January 5, 1945

No flying, except practice mission. We were told today we had to be at our gun stations from the time we take off until we land. A captured German gave the information that some time the Luftwaffe is going to attack us just as we take off or land. They've done it before. He claims they'll pull something that will wipe out half the bomber force in England. Ordinarily we used to get into our gun positions when we were across the channel.

We also know if we finish this tour we'll have to go to the C. B. I. Theater. I couldn't take another tour. I'm afraid I'm just about done for now.

Briol Mission No. 30, Group Mission No. 170,
Saturday, January 6, 1945

We helped the ground troops today as we've been doing on the last few missions. Our target was the marshalling yards of a little German town named Kempenich. It was pretty cloudy

168

over the target today but the whole town was destroyed. We bombed PFF (radar). We were doubly alert on our take off and landing today, keeping in mind the promise of that German pilot who said they were going to take us by surprise and wipe out half our bombers.

Our group saw no enemy fighters today. There was very little flak. I saw no planes go down. It gives me courage. There were a few Fortresses straggling over Germany but none of ours. We got up about three o'clock this morning, installed our guns by the light of the moon. On our way to Germany in the moonlight, our gas load was 2,500 gallons. Our bomb load was fourteen bombs, each weighing 500 lbs.

Over Germany we saw the vapor trails of many V-2 bombs headed for England. Germany was covered with heavy snow. Soon as we got to our own lines we dropped down to almost a thousand feet altitude, (very low). We saw plenty. We flew over Brussels, Belgium, then over the coast, (going home). We hit awful bad weather and were skimming the waves of the Channel all the way back to England, flying so low over battleships and destroyers in the Channel that we almost touched them. The weather was quite nice, over our base. It was clear. Got in pretty late this afternoon.

Spleth, Mission No. 32, Group Mission No. 170,
January 6, 1945 (Saturday), #4 high (591 W)
Target: Kempenich, Germany

Assembly and all O. K. No flak.

Came back under cloud deck and ran into some thick soup. Formation broke up and climbed up over it, clear over field, came in and landed O. K.

No battle damage. Supercharger on #2 went out on bomb run.

Briol, Sunday, January 7, 1945

Our crew didn't fly today. The Group did. It's snowing here in England today. Something unusual for England. I went to Mass and Communion this morning.

Our planes came back a little while ago. They supported the ground troops again. Our navigator finished his missions today. He'll be going home now. How lucky he is!

I was never so tense in my life. So many things could happen on these few missions I have left. These new guys in here still haven't flown their first mission. They turned out to be very nice fellows. I feel sorry for them. If the poor guys only knew what they have to go through.

We're on the loading list for tomorrow. I'm sweating it out, waiting for tomorrow's mission.

Briol, Monday, January 8, 1945

We didn't fly. Bad weather here and over the Continent. It's pretty cold, snowing a little. Our radio man and engineer flew this morning. They went over to Liverpool to get our Squadron Commander, Major Snow. Snow had Pat, the Red Cross girl, with him. She'd get in trouble if it was found out she rode in an army plane. It's none of our business.

The crew wants to go back to Spechtley, (flak house) on their next 48 hour pass. I don't think I will. When I'm through with my missions, I'd like to go up to North Ireland, but I don't think we'll be here long enough. I'd just as soon get out of here.

It's just been announced that the Germans may send a few buzz bombs over New York. Maybe it would be a good thing. It would wake the people up a little and let them have a taste of what we go through over here. It can be done. I'll predict that right now.

Briol, Tuesday, January 9, 1945

Although we were on the loading list last night, they changed it to a stand down, so our group did not fly today. It's snowing quite heavy now. Everything is icy. This is the most snow I've seen in five years. We're supposed to have a pass tomorrow but I'd sooner get these missions finished. I'm going crazy just waiting for them. I want to get home so darn bad. We had classes and lectures all day. Roads are so icy there must have been ten guys who fell off their bikes going down to classes. I was almost one of them.

There's a couple Fortresses circling the field waiting to come in.

I've found out what all these bomb bay tanks are doing on the field. I hope I'm through with my missions before we use them. They're going to be used for fire bombs to be dropped at low altitude. They hold 450 gallons of a very inflammable jelly like liquid, equipped with detonators. When dropped they explode and spread fire over a large area like a flame thrower. If we'd have to go in at low altitude with those things it would be suicide. Not one of us would reach the target without being blasted to bits by the Germans.

I learned today that Colonel Rogner, who was supposed to lead us over the target (but didn't), on the Bohlen raid near Leipzig, got a cluster for his D.F.C. Sure, he fell out, with one engine shot out and headed for home while he ordered us to go around again. It was we who hit the target through that hell, not he, and what do we get for it? Nothing. A lot of men died going over that second time. Of course, I realize that's war, but I'd still hate to have that on my conscience. We were mighty lucky to make it to Belgium.

There's still a heavy snowfall tonight.

Briol, Wednesday, January 10, 1945 (Group Mission No. 172)

We briefed to bomb the German city of Euskirchen, but our ship never got there. We were ready for the take-off early this morning and as we went roaring down the runway, two of our engines quit just as we were ready to leave the ground. Spleth cut the engines and used the brakes. The runway was full of ice and snow. We were prepared for the crash with our bomb load but we stopped just in time before going off the end of the runway. We carried all our equipment to the spare ship and took off again. We were a 100 miles behind the formation and couldn't catch up any more, so we turned back at the coast of Belgium. It would have been suicide to continue on alone because very few of the guns worked in the spare ship. Everything worked wrong. We worked for an hour trying to fix our guns. We explained our situation back at operations.

We got our 48 hour pass today. I don't feel like doing much. I'm going to get a good rest out of it.

Briol, Friday, January 12, 1945

Just came off pass. The rest of the crew went back to Spechtley. They aren't back yet. I went to a couple of dances at Du Jon's, and also took in a couple English movies. Slept until eleven o'clock at the Red Cross both mornings.

Briol, Saturday, January 13, 1945

Our crew didn't fly today. The rest did. They didn't get back to this base. They were diverted to some other field. It's foggy here again and raining. There's no more snow. An English Spitfire had to crash land here today. The pilot is okay.

Nick Benos, one of my best friends in the States is from this field. He finished his missions. His pal, Alfano, and also a good friend of mine, was killed over Germany. He was hit in the head by flak. Nick and Alfano were like two brothers. Back in the States, Nick was a very witty guy talking all the time. While over here he never said a word. He's getting back to normal again now that he's finished. I wish I was finished.

Briol, Mission No. 31, Group Mission No. 174, Sunday, January 14, 1945

Today, we destroyed the huge Cologne bridge over the Rhine River in Cologne, Germany, with thousand pound bombs. We got up early this morning. The Catholics received Communion and ate, then briefed. Each ship carried six 1,000 lb. bombs. The gas load was 2,600 gallons.

At altitude it was 45 degrees below zero. Our course was down to the southern tip of England, across the Channel, across Belgium into Germany. Our route was the same way coming back. We no sooner hit the enemy lines and they started blasting away at us and kept on all the way to Cologne and back. Several ships went down from our Group.

The other ships are not back from the last raid so we only put up twelve ships today. Jacob's crew was one that went down. One of the lead ships had its nose blown off and I think both men in the nose were dead. As for us, shrapnel passed through our ship in many places but spared all of our crew.

The flak was very accurate. Most of it was just exploding below us, practically in my face so to speak. The ship was thrown around a lot. You'd hear a tremendous "whump" and a concussion and usually a flash. You'd see those deadly puffs of smoke all over. Many times you'd hear a loud "clang" as a piece of shrapnel went ripping through the ship. We had two gas tanks punctured but they didn't leak much, (self sealing), four holes in the stabilizer and one through the waist. All this time I was as usual praying for my very life and the rest of the crew.

We got to the target with our bomb bay doors hanging open and Grybos still throwing chaff. "Bombs Away!" and our thousand pounders went screaming down on the Cologne bridge below. Flak was still bursting all over but I watched the bombs hit. There were concussion rings a couple blocks in diameter as the bombs hit on the bridge, around it and in the Rhine River. It was demolished and a huge pillar of black smoke hung over it. A large part of the city was hit too.

As another group of Fortresses came over in back of us. I saw they dropped their bombs in the same place. I saw the Cathedral of Cologne standing out from the rest of the city. Bombs hit near it but it looked like it was standing good yet. It was probably hit on other raids.

There was flak all the way back to the lines again. We evaded a lot of it. A lot of planes fell back straggling. Germany was covered with snow. No enemy fighters attacked us. Our fighters intercepted them before they could form over Germany. We started relaxing after we got to Belgium again. The snow started disappearing. By the time we got to England the snow was all gone.

An Englishman told me the snow we had here was the third in a hundred years. It's all melted now, though. England looks more lovely after every mission when we see it coming over the horizon. I imagine what America is going to look like when I see it again.

We took off in the dark this morning and we made it back in time for Mass tonight. Even got chow tonight. They actually had chicken. My back feels like it's going to ache for a week.

Although enemy fighters did not hit our group, they got through to some of the other groups. There were 180 enemy fighters shot down. Over 30 enemy fighters were shot down by the bombers. I don't know how many bombers were lost. I hate to think of it.

Spleth, Mission No. 33, Group Mission No. 174,
January 14, 1945 (Sunday), #4 Lead (591 W)
Target: Cologne, Germany

We went into the back door of Cologne today. I was leading the low element of the low section which was only 748th ships. The 457th only put up one box today.

We hit flak three times today. First at the lines going in, then at the target and at the lines on return. Flak was very accurate. Returned O. K.

Battle damage--hole near #3 nacelle, had to take out tank to patch; skin ripped left side navigation compartment. Everyone O. K.

Briol, Monday, January 15, 1945

There was a mission for today but they scrubbed it. There'll be a practice mission this afternoon. The guns have to be manned even on practice missions now, for fear of enemy fighters.

Briol, Tuesday, January 16, 1945

We briefed today for the bombing of "BIG B" (Berlin) but it was scrubbed as we were about to take-off. My hand is shaking today. I can hardly write. It's very foggy again today. I had trouble sleeping last night although I was tired. I just lay awake smoking, with horrible thoughts in my mind.

Briol, Mission No. 32
Group Mission No. 175, Wednesday, January 17, 1945

Our target for today was the railroad aqueduct of Alkenbekon, near to Munster, Germany. Our bomb load was six 1,000 lb. bombs. Gas load was 2,780 gallons. The temperature was 40 degrees below zero Centigrade at high altitude. Our route was over the Channel, Holland and into Germany.

As we hit the Zuider Zee in Holland we ran into a flak barrage. It was cloudy and they didn't do so good with radar. Before the target we ran into another heavy barrage which was closer and a few ships were hit but I saw none of our group fall.

We didn't make a good run over the target, so Mueller ordered us to do a 360 and go around again. It wasn't so bad because there was very little flak over the target.

As our huge bombs went down to the target our ship jumped because it had been lightened so quick. We sent them out in salvo. The target was clouded over, so I didn't see what damage we did. We turned around and headed for home, tense and on guard against enemy fighters. They didn't attack us.

It seemed like it took us all day to get out of Heinie land. We were bucking a 90 mile an hour head wind. It seemed like we'd never get out. As we hit the coast of Holland we ran into another flak barrage. We used a lot of evasive action. I don't think anyone got hit there. They came plenty close, though.

Some how I have a lot of respect for the R.A.F. They don't bomb in daylight like we do but they've been hitting some mighty tough targets. They've been losing quite a few ships and men on them too. I've watched them go over scattered all over the sky. They don't go over in formation. It's mostly individual bombing. They never used to publish their losses like we do.

I've often wondered how many of our airmen are lying dead over in Germany unidentified. Some don't even reach the ground if they're blown to bits or cremated in their Flying Fortresses. Like at Magdeburg when we saw over a 100 highly trained airmen die while you snap your fingers. I'll never get that raid off my mind. Every time a Fortress goes down, nine men to with it. I hate to say it but we've gone on raids in which I was positive I'd never come back.

I don't know what keeps us from backing out. I guess it's all the men together. You know what each one on your crew is capable of. Each member keeps the other going. You look at the rest of your crew, they're not going to back out, so neither am I.

It's like a grab bag. You ride through a solid wall of flak, or hit fighters. You know someone is going down. You don't know who. When you go over the target with heavy flak, the Germans can't miss the whole formation. Someone has to get it. Everyone is hoping it's not them but someone always gets it. You also know, many more men are praying like yourself.

Spleth, Mission No. 34, Group Mission No. 175
January 17, 1945 (Wednesday)
Target: Paderborn, Germany

Not much on this one. Col. Francis led. Ran into soup and climbed like hell. Managed to keep in formation O. K. Climbed above briefed altitude, then let down just before I. P. Made a run on the target, but for some d___ reason we didn't drop--hit a little flak on run.

Well, we made a 360, very tight, and dropped bombs. Dam near shuffled with another group--came back O. K. Hans and Fritz took a crack at us. Landed O. K.

Briol, Thursday, January 18, 1945

The mission was scrubbed for today. It's raining quite heavy now and there's a high wind. The mud and rain are rolling in under our bunks again. I'm glad I've got an upper bunk. We're trying to fix our stove. Supposed to have lectures this afternoon. Have to get out of it some way. There's no warmth around here.

Maybe I'll go down to the lecture. They have a stove down there. Boy, is it raining! Karl Lambertson our waist gunner, is on flak leave now. He'll probably be back with us to fly with us on our last missions. Harry may get in his extra mission tomorrow. Harry has four to go. The rest of us have three to go, except Spleth, who has just one. Those three seem like a hundred.

Briol, Friday, January 19, 1945

Stand down all night. No flying. I thought the wind was going to blow our shack down last night. There's a dance at the Aero Club tonight. I might go over.

Briol, Saturday, January 20, 1945

Our crew didn't fly but our group went out. There was an accident when the planes came back. One ship came in with a feathered prop and a locked wheel. It nosed over and crashed

176

in the center of the runway.

It was from the 750th squadron. Most of the crew was dead, as for the rest of the planes, I don't have to say much. The ambulances were mighty busy. Two men I knew were killed. Both were hit in the head. A radio man had all his teeth knocked out and it came out the back of his head. The other, a bombardier, had a piece of flak go through the left side of his head and out the right side. I'm not used to seeing things like that but we accept it.

Briol, Mission No. 33, Group Mission No. 177
Sunday, January 21, 1945

Our target for today was the German tank works of a small city named Aschaffenburg. It's southeast of Frankfurt. We made a long trip out of it. Our gas load was 2,600 gallons. We carried twelve 500 lb. bombs and some incendiaries.

It was about 50 degrees below zero at altitude (Centigrade). Lots of vapor trails. Our route was to the southern tip of England over London, the Channel, the whole length of France into Germany. There we headed north and snuck in, so to speak. We ran into flak close to Stuttgart but it was inaccurate. There was very little over the target.

We supported the ground troops. I didn't see the damage because it was covered by clouds. We used radar to bomb.

As we left the target our No. 2 engine sprang an oil leak and lost all its oil. We had to feather it. No. 3 was over heating and back firing. It kept going although we had to leave formation and straggle. We got back to England alone tonight. (Sunday). We sweated out the landing because No. 3 was flashing now and then and we were afraid it would catch fire.

Spleth, Mission No. 35! Group Mission No. 177,
January 21, 1945, #4 Low (506)
Target: Aschaffenburg, Germany

Weather was a little stinky. We flew in clouds on climb over Channel.

Went into target O.K. No flak or fighters; got rid of bombs O. K. Feathered #2, #3 caught on fire 25 miles from field, let the d___ thing burn. Made an emergency landing,

firing flares on the approach like mad.
No battle damage.

THE END.

HOORAY!

Welch, January 22, 1945

Lauren Spleth flew his 35th and last mission yesterday. Hooray for him!

Ted Braffmann flew with another crew, to bomb Bitburg, on January 7, and that was his 35th and last.

Tragedy struck the crew today. Lambertson, trying to gain a mission and thus finish sooner, flew today as a fill-in gunner with Jellinek and crew to bomb a place called Sterkrade. They didn't come back.

We're still a crew. I'm the first pilot, and we still have Ozenberger, Haynes, Grybos, Briol and Cornell. When we fly, we'll fill in with a new or spare pilot, a spare bombardier, and a spare waist gunner. Ozzie, Grybos, Briol and I have two missions to go, Haynes and Cornell have three.

CHAPTER XIII

BERLIN, WE'RE COMING

Briol, Monday, January 22, 1945, Group Mission No. 178

Our crew didn't fly today. There was to be a mission but I think it was scrubbed. Some planes took off but I think it was a practice mission. It's snowing again.

There _was_ a mission today. They encountered heavy flak over the target. Several of our ships did not return. Karl Lambertson, our waist gunner, flew with Jellinek's crew today and he did not come back. The other crews saw them get hit but it's still possible they made it to friendly territory. Lambertson was a swell guy and I'm hoping. His whole crew was shot down over Germany, that's why he's on our crew now. Most of us have two to go. We have a new navigator. Lambertson was about ten missions behind us. Spleth is finished up on our crew now. We'll have another pilot for the last two, to take Spleth's place. (Ed. note: Welch took over the crew.)

The ships were pretty badly shot up again today.

I have two more missions to put in but it seems like a hundred. So many things could happen. After getting this far, I have to finish these two, that's all there is to it. I have to cheat death twice more and then I can go home for a while. It doesn't seem possible that I once led a normal life.

I have a strange feeling though, if I have to go to the Pacific and fly, something is going to happen. I guess I just can't take it. I'm in agony every time I see a burst of flak now. I'm not the only one, though. Ozzie told me the other day how scared he was. Every man on the crew thinks he's the most scared. I'll stick to my duty as long as I can but I guess even the most stout can give only so much.

Briol, Tuesday, January 23, 1945

We were awakened this morning by five buzz bombs exploding nearby. Our field had a stand down all night, so no one flew today. We had the usual classes and lectures. We'll probably get one more 48 hour pass before we finish up.

179

There were a great number of men killed this afternoon at a base near here, when a B-17 loaded with 500 lb. bombs exploded near some barracks. We heard the explosion.

My bunk is occupying the same space that Petty used to occupy. I can still remember before he went down, how he used to get his rations at the P. X. He couldn't sleep good at night (neither could I) and I could hear him eating cookies or something at all hours of the night.

Two men have finished up on Zeiler's crew. They are the first to finish up and go home from this hut.

No word from Karl Lambertson, our waist gunner, yet. He always used to meet a little French girl at Du Jon's when he went to town. I suppose we'll have to tell her.

Briol, Wednesday, January 24, 1945

Stand down again. Bad weather, lectures this afternoon. Karl is now missing in action. We don't know if he's dead or not. He's another man on our crew that came to a bad end. About the nicest fellow I ever knew. Stand down tonight, so we won't fly tomorrow. Going to Peterborough to rest my nerves.

Briol, Saturday, January 27, 1945

We just came off pass. The whole crew (what's left of us) went to Peterborough and slept at the Red Cross. Went to a couple English shows and one dance at Du Jon's. Hitch hiked in and took a civilian bus back.

Briol, Sunday, January 28, 1945

Today is the anniversary of the 8th Air Force but I didn't fly. It's just as well because the Luftwaffe is liable not to be idle today. The rest of our Group flew but they're not back yet.

It's quite cold today. Fresh snow on the ground, can't get any coal. Can't destroy the King's trees, so I guess we'll just have to be miserable. Went to Mass at the theater this morning. Ice all over the floor where the water ran in and froze.

Welch is up on a practice mission right now. I'm going down to the line and sweat the rest of the guys in from the raid.

180

I watched them come in. They hit Cologne today (again). Four of the ships were shot up some but there was nothing real serious. Makes a guy feel good although one ship from the 749th was lost over the target. It was Boye's crew. They had only a couple missions to go.

Briol, Monday, January 29, 1945 Group Mission No. 180

We were supposed to fly today but they changed the loading list this morning. We spent the morning at turret trainer and lectures. No information about Karl, our waist gunner, except that other crews reported seeing the ship that Karl was flying in (Jellinek's crew) fall over the target with its tail shot off. They didn't see anyone bail out.

Briol, Tuesday, January 30, 1945

Stand down all night, so we didn't fly. There was a heavy snow and it melted this afternoon. Our hut is practically washed away. There's so many men missing on our crew now that it's liable to make spare gunners out of us. There's only five of us left of the original crew we came over with.

Briol, Wednesday, January 31, 1945

We briefed to bomb BIG B (Berlin) itself again today. The fog rolled in just as we were about to take off and I was glad. We would have run into enemy fighters today. Plenty of them.

It was about six o'clock this morning when we got back to the hut, so we slept for a while. Had a bunch of films and lectures later. We're still classed as a crew. We'll be using spare gunners to complete it.

We were told today that if we had any scruples about bombing civilians, it was hard luck for us because from now on we'll be bombing and strafing women, children, everybody. I'm glad I've only got a few more to do. So far, most of our raids were at military objectives but you can't destroy objectives without losing lives on both sides.

Briol, Mission No. 34
Thursday, February 1, 1945, Group Mission No. 181

Today we bombed Ludwigshafen, Germany, again. It was an easier run this time than the last time we went there. There was less flak this time. We carried 500 lb. bombs and some incendiaries. Our gas load was 2,780 gallons.

Going in we crossed the Channel, the whole length of France and then into Germany.

As we went over the fighting lines, we saw two chutes open. They started drifting down. I didn't see any plane falling, so I'm still stymied.

As we neared the target they blasted away at us. Most of it exploded harmlessly below us. There were a few that came close to us. The low box got hit some. We couldn't see the damage we did because of clouds. We finally got out of the flak and headed south right to the border of Switzerland to throw off enemy fighters. Then we headed northwest back over France, the Channel and home.

I had a terrific headache today. I felt like I wanted to die. I'm so darn tired, I can't keep my eyes open now.

Pat, the Ball Turret gunner on Zeiler's crew, flew with a brand new crew. The tail gunner saw a Fortress fall over the target and he started screaming over the interphone.

Ozenberger, Mission No. 34
February 1, 1944

My next to last mission was to Ludwigshafen, Germany, and we didn't have much flak, and no fighters. The main reason that I am writing about the mission is that I sweat it out so much. It has been about two weeks since we flew our 33rd mission (the one that Spleth finished on), and I was getting rather jumpy. Very close to going home. The mission was a long mission, around eight or nine hours. There was very little flak over the target when we got there. The flak came up while we were there but it was all low. After we were over the target a lot of flak came up but we were gone and it didn't bother. The Group behind got it, though.

I flew waist for the first time. I hope I don't do it again, I was sure scared.

Briol, February 2, 1945

We briefed for Berlin again today but it was scrubbed. We were going to help the Russian troops. We would have bombed and killed many of the evacuees coming out of Berlin and Dresden. I'm afraid we'd have lots of losses too.

We took our guns and equipment back and went back to sleep for a while. I've got to put everything I've got into my next mission because it's going to be my last raid here in Europe. I've got to come back from that one. There's just one mission standing between me and going home. One more mission and this nightmare will be over. It's going to be safe to think about home, Marcella and all the things I've missed. If only I can put in an easier raid than what we were briefed today. I go mad when I think about it.

The Russians don't even know what an American uniform looks like. I doubt if they know a Fortress. We were told, if we were crippled and made it to Russia, about the only thing we could do is bail out and take our chances because, undoubtedly Russian fighters and flak would intercept us. We have not got a code between us and the Russians yet. So far, we may be able to prove we're friendly by dipping the wings or firing a white flare.

We have to watch our step because they are not taking German prisoners. They kill them as fast as they can. Even if we parachuted and they thought we were German we'd be dead before we'd reach the ground. We have our plans for escape and evasion if we touch German soil alive. There's a lot of confusion in Germany now and it's to our advantage. I have my plan in my head.

Briol, Mission No. 35!
Saturday, February 3, 1945, Group Mission No. 182

I finished my last mission today but it was a rough one, right to the heart of Berlin. We were briefed early this morning (3 o'clock) to bomb Berlin. It was not to be an industrial target but for the sole purpose of killing people to break the morale of the Germans.

I'm not proud of this raid. I'm afraid it will be on my conscience until the day I die. Anyway, I'm still alive and I'm so very grateful I don't know whether to laugh or cry.

The whole 8th Air Force pounded this target. I watched them go over, group after group. Our group was seventh over the target. Some of the Luftwaffe was up after us but before they got to our group, our fighter pilots shot them down without mercy. I've never seen such slaughter. It was a visual run and we had lots of casualties, too. By the time we got to the target there were great pillars of smoke rising from the center of Berlin.

There were 3,000,000 refugees down there. We lost 40 bombers. What a horrible thing to finish up on. I pity any of our men who had to bail out and got to the ground alive. If they were caught, they were probably cut to pieces by the Germans.

We took off early this morning while it was still dark. Each ship carried ten 500 lb. bombs. Our gas load was 2,700 gallons. It was 40 degrees below zero over the target. We headed out over the North Sea. As we hit the coast of Holland, the flak started bursting around us but we used evasive action and it didn't get any of us, as far as I could see. We skirted all flak areas until we hit central Germany, then some more burst around us but we didn't get hit. It was a long trip.

After hours of flying we hit the I. P. and started down the bomb run. Our bomb bay doors came open. I was scared stiff on this last mission. We just had to make it.

We were getting close to the target now. I could see Berlin below, smoking and exploding from the groups ahead of us. I looked up in front of us and saw the smoke markers going down. The sky was black with flak bursts and the bombers flying through them. There were two tremendous explosions ahead of us as two Fortresses got hit and blew to bits right in front of us. Another got hit and went down in a steep dive. Half the men bailed out and went floating down into the fire and smoke.

Now it was our turn. We were getting into the flak now and I never prayed so loud and long before. We heard two explosions in front of us. None of the fragments hit us. There were a bunch of explosions to our left but they still didn't hit us. There must have been about ten explosions directly underneath us. We heard fragments penetrating the wings and gas tanks from those but no gas leaked out because of the self sealing tanks. At the same time we dropped our bombs and made a

184

steep turn to the right.

Giessen's crew from the 749th at this base was hit by those last flak bursts and his ship went spinning right down into the center of Berlin. I didn't see anyone get out and neither did anyone else. I think that was the only ship that went down from this field here. We were mighty lucky.

We made another sharp turn, to the left, and a flak burst appeared just where we would have been if we'd have gone straight. We made some more turns to evade the flak. It was mostly bursting below us now. As we went over the Russians, they fired at us and I think we lost some there.

We turned around and started for home. Although we were hit a little, none of our engines were hit and none of the crew got hit. We called an oxygen check to see if everyone was okay. Our bomb bay doors came up now and I was thanking God.

As we turned around I watched the group behind us going over the target and I saw two more Fortresses blow up from flak. They must have got it right in their bombs. At first I thought they were two great flak bursts but they looked like two big red balls of fire that went billowing out in all directions. There wasn't even a little piece left.

As we got back to the central part of Germany we had to leave our formation and lose altitude because our oxygen was leaking somewhere and it was getting low. We were low enough to do damage with our machine guns. Our navigator knew where all the flak areas were, so we went around them all. They shot at us but we evaded it. Since it was our last mission we were shooting at everything that suggested enemy troops and installations, just saving enough ammunition in case we were attacked by fighters.

We weren't too worried though because our fighter planes on the way back were protecting us. A string of our fighters would go by and come in close and look at us to see our plane was still okay. Flak started bursting again as we hit the coast of Holland but we evaded it again.

As we hit the North Sea again, we all relaxed. We had done it again and we took our last look at Heinie Land. I was dead tired but I was so happy I sang to myself all the way across the North Sea. That was four more of our crew now that finished up, myself, Ozzie, Welch and Grybos. Harry and

Haynes still are not finished. The rest of our crew were men who replaced those who are not with us any more. I kissed the English soil when I got out of the ship, I was so glad to be back after this last one.

I found out the father of Giessen was back here waiting for that crew to come back but they didn't come back. Giessen's father was a colonel and he came over yesterday to visit him.

I've got a headache and I can still hear the roar of engines in my ears, So I'm going to hit the sack.

Ozenberger, Mission No. 35!
February 3, 1945, Group Mission No. 182

My last mission was to Berlin (Big B) on the third of February. We had been briefed for it three days in a row before we finally made it. I sure didn't want it. It is the largest target there is. We were to bomb it visually. That is bad.

The whole 8th Air Force was out. We sure plastered the target. We dropped them right in the center of the city. The flak wasn't too bad, not what we expected. We got only one hole, in our left wing.

We didn't see any fighters, but they were up. I don't see how they missed us. I don't know of any mission I ever sweat out so much. My interphone went out just before the bomb run and I couldn't hear. So I opened the bomb bay doors and dropped the bombs, without hearing anyone talk, on the Lead's smoke marker.

We dropped ten 500 pound bombs on people that couldn't protect themselves. I don't call that war.

On the way back we ran out of oxygen, so we had to leave the formation, so then we were on our own again. But nothing came at us, so got back to the base all safe and sound.

Briol, Grybos, Welch and I were the only ones that finished on that mission. Haynes and Cornell had one left to go. (Their last mission was flown on the 5th of February and they returned safely.) This completed our tour of duty in the European Theater of War, and we were homeward bound.

Welch, Mission No. 35, Group Mission No. 182, Aircraft 101
February 3, 1945, Target: Berlin; High Element Lead

186

Today, February 3, 1945, has been the saddest day of my life. The whole 8th Air Force bombed Berlin today. The city is filled with refugees fleeing from the advancing Russian army. There's no possible way for all those people to find bomb shelters or any other protection from bombs. God, help them.

We were briefed to bomb the Friedrichstrasse Railroad Station area, with the aiming point a bridge over the Spree River.

The target area was clear, and we were about the seventh group to bomb the city. I could see all the groups ahead as they went in, and all those following as we turned away from the target. It's terrible to think about what it must been like on the ground.

I've been the crew commander and first pilot on this mission and the one to Ludwigshafen two days ago. Six of our original crew flew both missions. Ozenberger, Briol, Grybos and I flew our 35th missions today; Haynes and Cornell, who each lost a mission because of illness, will probably fly their last ones on the next Group mission.

Thank God--I don't have to drop bombs on anyone else, at least for a while. Thank Him, also, that the four of us, as well as Spleth, Byknish and Braffmann, won't be getting shot at any more, at least for a while.

We're very worried about Karl Lambertson, and would surely like to hear some positive news about him. Is he at least a POW?

Our crew began flying combat missions on last September 12. Beginning then, the Group has flown 62 missions, we've flown 35 for credit, had two mechanical aborts, and flew as spare once or twice. Longest mission was to Politz, 9:45. Four others were 9:00 or longer. We lost a total of twelve engines due to battle damage or mechanical failures, about an 8 1/2 percent rate based on four engines exposed each mission, or .34 engines per mission. We were assigned an airplane, 591W, and managed to get thirteen missions in it. We flew fifteen other B-17's on combat missions, three each in 101, 394 and 506, two each in 537 and 954, and one each in 051, 219, 479, 583, 606, 662, 751, 796, 899, and 905. We got back to base in all of them except 583, which we left at Mons, Belgium returning from the mission to Bohlen.

It has been a dreadful way "to earn a living". I <u>have</u>

enjoyed flying for orientation of new pilots, slow-timing engines, and simply flying landing practice in the traffic pattern.

I have been offered immediate promotion to Captain, flying primarily with lead crews, if I'll come back to the Squadron after 30 days leave at home. I said "No, thank you." I've had enough here. I plan to volunteer for B-29's, and the Squadron Ops. Officer gave me a written recommendation for training into them. So, for now I'll go home and try to forget all about this stuff.

The sulfa pills must work--I haven't had a cold the whole time I've been taking them.

CHAPTER XIV

WINDING DOWN - HOMEWARD BOUND

John Briol's Account from here on

February 4, 1945

Today is Sunday, I slept till ten o'clock, then went to Mass at the theater. It's a beautiful day today. The sun is out and it's nice and warm. It reminds me of a spring day in Minnesota. I feel like living once more. I just can't quite believe that I can go home now. I'm mighty grateful to be one of the few who come back from their raids. When I got back yesterday, I just knelt in the chapel over an hour, I was so grateful.

It's hard to go back, though, realizing that so many of my buddies are dead over Germany. There were many times when I was almost sure I wouldn't come back out of Germany again, but here I am, a free man once more.

February 5, 1945

We didn't do much today except lie around and wait for our orders to come through. Our orders came through. We'll leave for Stone again this coming Friday. We'll be there for a while and then we'll probably go back to the States by boat. Myself, Ozzie and Grybos will be together. Harry, our tail gunner and Haynes our Top Turret gunner have not finished their missions. I'm hoping they'll finish before we leave.

I turned in all my flying equipment this afternoon and went all over the base getting my clearance slip checked off, etc. I wanted to take my trusty .45 pistol with me but I'm going to turn it in. I'll be able to get one in the states somewhere. That pistol gets to be a part of a man.

If only we hadn't lost Karl, our waist gunner, I'd be a much happier guy. I haven't quite figured out how I'm going to slip this combat diary out of England but there must be some way.

February 6, 1945

We're going to get a pass (the three of us) while we're waiting to ship out. We're going to spend it in Peterborough. It's raining quite hard now. It's going to be wonderful to be on pass and not have to worry about coming back to fly over Germany. Harry and Haynes went out on their last mission today. I'm going down to the line to sweat them out and wait for them to come back. They should be back by five o'clock.

It was a disastrous day. Harry and Haynes did not come back yet. No one saw their ship go down, though, so they must be all right somewhere. I could just feel it in my bones something was going to happen.

The ships couldn't even see the runway. They'd make a pass and go around again, just missing the buildings.

Major Doherty and his whole crew were killed trying to come in. (Ed. note--this was a test hop). We were watching him make his last turn on the approach. He was too low but he made a steep bank anyway. He must have hit prop wash because his left wing dropped on the turn and it was sheared off as it hit the ground. The Fortress was blazing before the rest of the ship hit. There was an explosion and the whole ship was covered with flames that rose to about a 100 feet into the air. Three ambulances raced out but no one could even get close to it.

Another ship came in and overshot. They slammed on the brakes, skidding all the way to the end of the runway, and ended up in the mud. No one was hurt there. Before anyone else came in they ordered the rest to land at some other field.

February 8,1945

We came back from pass. While on pass we found out at the Red Cross that Harry and Haynes were all right. They ran low on gas when they hit the coast of England and landed at some other base. When I saw that plane crash, I thought it was the plane they were in for a while.

We've all packed up ready to leave. We leave tomorrow morning.

February 10, 1945

We're back at Stone again, this time we're at Nelson Hall. We got in yesterday by train. Today we had a clothing check. We went to the dispensary for shots. It will be some time before we leave here for a port of embarkation. I'm not sure yet if we'll go by boat or fly. We'll be on a work detail tomorrow. We'll also have to get K. P. here. It's something to keep our minds and bodies occupied.

My appetite is starting to come back again. I really was hungry yesterday for the first time in a long time. Life is worth while again. Ozzie is lying in his bunk right now. He has two welts under his eyes caused by his oxygen mask while flying. I guess mine have disappeared. I lost a lot of weight but I guess I'm putting some back on again.

This paper war gets a guy down. Every time we go to a different place, there are forms and blanks and everything else to fill out. Too much red tape but I guess we're just the gypsies of the Army. We never have a permanent settlement, which suits me, I guess.

February 12, 1945

;

We've been on a few work details in the last couple days. Haven't had any K. P. yet. The three of us are still together. At night everyone has nightmares, it seems. One guy was calling out "Flak!", all night last night.

February 13, 1945

The three of us were on K. P. today. It wasn't so bad, though, because we worked in the dining room. We sat around and chewed the fat mostly. They're really not hard on men coming back from combat. We get these details because right now we are casuals and we have no job in the Army. It seems funny to see these veteran flyers doing these jobs, all with high ranks. We don't kick much. We're just glad to be alive.

The permanent parties around here respect us quite a bit, officers and all. They know we didn't have an easy time and we've seen things they'll never see. Here at Nelson Hall all the combat flyers that come in here are going home. We are the survivors. I'd say there are about three crews out of ten that survive.

February 14, 1945

We didn't do a darn thing today except loaf and lie around. Put our room into inspection order. That's all. This is a beautiful part of England around here by Stone. There are beautiful rolling hills and they are all green now. It's chilly today but the sun is out. It's lovely and quiet. No airplane engines roaring in our ears. There are a few WAC's at this place. They're permanent personnel. I don't know what their jobs are. I'd be the most happy man in the world, now, if the South Pacific weren't staring me in the face. I'm also going to be very happy, regardless, if a certain little lady agrees to something when I get home.

February 15, 1945

We were on a work detail today. I met some other gunners and we had quite a time exchanging experiences. They had been over in Belgium about the same time we were there. The conversation finally drifted around to some dead decomposed bodies we saw over there. We usually end an unpleasant conversation in quick time. I may as well add that those bodies were from a strafing raid.

I forgot to mention I saw Jimmy Stewart, the movie actor, over here a short time ago. He's a C. O. and pilot of a Liberator. He used to be with the 389th. He's with the second division now (Liberators). I don't think he's taking it so good. He's nervous and his hair is turning gray. He only has in about 18 missions and he started them before I left the states.

Some gunners came in from Switzerland yesterday. They were forced down there more than a year ago. They're going home, too. I'd write some letters but I don't know how long I'll be here. I've got combat fatigue or something and it seems to stick with me. I get very irritable moods, too.

February 16, 1945

Still waiting for orders to ship home. Ozzie has left for the States by plane. Grybos and I are still together. It seems hard to part with fellows like that after being together so long and going through almost death together. Grybos and I worked in the mess hall again today. Worked in the serving line. Easy job.

February 17, 1945

Grybos and I didn't do a thing today except lie around.

February 18, 1945

The two of us are on shipping orders now. It will be a few days before we ship out. We'll go back by boat. Have to wear leggings, steel helmet and everything else when we leave here. Didn't have anything to do today (Sunday) except a short work detail.

I hate some of these details. Some of them are really filthy. (One thing, when we were in combat, we never did anything except fly and fight and bomb, etc.) We had to carry around dirty mattresses and things from the officers' quarters today. Some officers come in drunk and they can't hold their drink like most enlisted men and they sure leave a mess on the bed clothes. I took a complete bath afterwards.

Is it any wonder why men get bitter in the army? Another thing, some of these filthy bed clothes are hauled out of the officers' quarters and given to the enlisted men, while the officers get clean stuff. I've never exaggerated anything in this diary yet. There were many things while I was in combat that I was under oath not to mention, so I didn't write it down.

It's very warm out again today and those rolling hills around here look greener than ever. I can truthfully say that England is beautiful now. I don't have to look forward to death for a while, but instead I look forward to home, so I just look around me and drink in this beauty. It's very quiet around here. Very few planes around to bring back memories. It's strange how when a man survives combat, he wants just the simplest luxuries in life. Anyway those are my feelings. It's a miracle in itself when a man survives thirty five combat missions. All the rest of the airmen from Switzerland will come in tonight, repatriated. Some of them have been interned for years.

February 20, 1945

I didn't do anything today but a lot of the men that came in from Switzerland are on details. I think I have about three days here yet. I go on guard duty tonight at 8 o'clock. I get off at midnight, eat, sleep and go on at eight in the morning again.

February 21, 1945

Got off guard duty a half hour ago. I had a lonely post last night. While I was walking my post, I was thinking of all sorts of things. I was thinking how I'd like to be out of this war and on the ground. I've seen too much happen. It's not much fun to see a riddled plane come back and see some poor guy's intestines splattered all over the inside and the rest of the crew crying like babies. When I have time on my hands, it seems as if I can't get away from the things I've seen.

As I walked along some rabbits would run out in front of me and it would take my mind off things. I got my ration card and went over to the P. X. to get my rations.

I'm going to get a pass tonight and go to a dance at one of the other halls. It won't be long until I can change my money into good old American money again. We're always paid in English money over here.

This place is really packed, now that all these men came in from Switzerland.

February 22, 1945

I'm hoping I'll be alerted today or tomorrow.

February 24, 1945

I just read in Stars and Stripes that we killed over 25,000 people in our last raid on Berlin on February 3rd.

I've been alerted now. We were supposed to ship out tonight at midnight but it has been delayed. Got my clearance signed and my money changed to American money, also had a "short arm". I'm all packed, ready to go. Had roll call a short while ago.

About that February 3rd raid on Berlin, we also destroyed the hated Gestapo headquarters and many other places. I hate to think of the innocent people that had to die, though.

194

February 25, 1945

We're supposed to eat at eleven thirty tonight and ship out at twelve thirty. Went to Mass today (Sunday). That's about all I did worth mentioning.

February 26, 1945

We are now on board ship to leave port. This is Southampton, England. We're quite far below. We spent most of the night on the train and arrived here about noon. They're taking on a lot of wounded, a lot in mighty bad shape. The name of this ship is "The General Gordon". Tonight it was suffocating below deck, so I went up and walked all over the ship. Watched the huge cranes loading cargo. There are a lot of guns on this ship, antiaircraft, etc. We'll probably leave port tomorrow, maybe join a convoy. They've worried about enemy submarines.

February 27, 1945

We left port today but we're still in the harbor forming the convoy. We might as well be classified as navy men as long as we're on this ship. It's run by the Navy and we pull our details and work with the rest of the sailors. I'm getting a taste of Navy life.

We have 72 prisoners on this ship.

The wounded coming back on this boat are looked after mostly by the medics. We sometimes help those who can walk when they go to the mess hall. There are all kinds. Some without arms, legs, some are without eyes. A lot of these are infantry. You don't see quite so many in the Air Corps who are wounded. The flyers either come back or they're killed all the way. On the ground when you're wounded, there's someone to take care of you. In the air your ship can go down if you're wounded, oxygen mask fall off, freeze, a hundred things.

I'm glad a convoy of ships are going back together. I don't want to get torpedoed now after getting through everything else. There are ships anchored all around us out in the harbor. I'm sure we'll pull out of the harbor tomorrow.

February 28, 1945

There are still ships joining us in the harbor. I miss the rest of the crew. I'm playing that lone wolf hand once again. Even the officers pull duty on this ship.

March 1, 1945

Fourth day on this ship and we're still in the harbor. The water was pretty rough today. It's foggy, too. I imagine the water will really be rough when we get out to sea. We'll have to wear life jackets most of the time.

There have been fights among the prisoners already.

Now I know what good eats the Navy gets. I've never had eats like this all the time I've been in the Army.

The main deck rises above the water about the height of an ordinary house. In rough weather there will be waves coming over it. We had abandon ship drill today. The sister ship to this one is anchored off our port side. There was an inspection by the ship's captain today.

March 2, 1945

We pulled out of the harbor about noon today. We're well out to sea now. The ship is starting to rock quite a bit. I hope the sea gets rough. I like it that way.

I guess there are about 15 ships all spaced out about a half mile apart. Some destroyers are escorting us. It isn't quite so stuffy below deck. It's cold up on the main deck. Had abandon ship drill and will probably get it tonight. These ships are like floating cities.

March 3, 1945

The water was kind of rough today. A lot of the men are getting sea-sick. One of the toughest prisoners (at least he thinks he's tough) was sea-sick and spilled his guts right in the mess hall. The guards made him clean it up, too.

Two flat tops (aircraft carriers) have joined us. We still have our four destroyer escort.

I was on a detail today, but tomorrow I have free. I love

to lie in my bunk at night and feel the ship rock and sometimes hear the steel plates groaning. It rocks me to sleep every night.

March 4, 1945.

Seventh day on the boat. I didn't have anything to do today (Sunday). I went to Mass up in the officer's lounge. I spent most of the morning up on deck watching the waves go by. The sea is getting rougher and more guys are getting sea-sick. The weather looks kind of bad. It's starting to rain a little.

Just came down from a movie in No. 3 hold. It was a good movie, not taking into consideration we sat on the floor and I had seen it twice before.

I don't know for sure, yet, but we'll probably dock in Norfolk, Virginia. I was hoping it would be New York. I think we'll get to the States by the 14th of March. I used to take the ferry boat over to Norfolk when I was at Langley Field.

March 5, 1945

I'm on detail again today. The ocean is still rough but it looks as if the sun might come out. Our four destroyers are still with us, zig-zagging back and forth looking for submarines. These ships can outrun a sub but they could be lying waiting for us. After going through 35 missions, submarines don't worry me much.

March 6, 1945

I have nothing to do today. I was up on deck for a while early this morning. The white caps are breaking alongside of the ship and they send a salt water spray up on deck. One of the flat tops is directly behind us now. These flat tops have no planes on them as far as I can see. Our destroyers are still zig-zagging out in the distance. Our bunks are halfway hanging bunks made of canvas. Something like a hammock, except they have a steel re-inforcer all around them. The sun is shining now, and it's really warm up on deck. It's very windy, though, and the waves are pretty high. I saw another movie in No. 3 hold. Each day is bringing me closer to America. It still doesn't seem possible that I'm going home.

March 7, 1945

Tenth day on the boat. I'm working in the mess hall today, on the serving line. We're practically working our way across the ocean. I have to get back on the job in about an hour.

The ocean was the roughest so far last night. We ran into a little squall. It woke me up several times.

March 8, 1945

There's quite a gale blowing today. We can't go up on deck without being salted from head to foot. That salt water spray goes over everything. I haven't a thing to do today. If the movie projector wasn't broken, I'd go to a movie.

I just came down from the front of the ship before turning in for the night. It quit raining but it's blowing hard and it's cold. The waves were coming almost over the front of the ship. It rises and falls. There's one tanker in the convoy. I don't see how it stays afloat. I don't think anyone can even go on deck on it. The front dips into the water and it looks as if the whole thing goes under for a while. We're heading into this wind and it's slowing us down quite a bit. You can hardly walk up on deck right now.

This is about a 25,000 ton ship. Its sister ship is the same size and it's off to our starboard.

Well, I'm going to let the ship rock me to sleep again.

March 9, 1945

Twelfth day on the boat. Another fight on board today (bloody).

The sun comes out for five minutes, then it disappears and it starts raining. It's still quite cold up on deck.

It's getting rough aboard this ship. There was another fight this noon, among the prisoners this time.

We're going to have another ship's inspection. It was announced that our destination was to be New York after all.

March 10, 1945

It's raining and foggy on the ocean today but it's not

198

quite so cold. The water isn't quite so rough, either.

I'm worried, I haven't heard from Marcella for a long time. I wish I knew what was going on. I always have thoughts that she'll be sent somewhere else and she won't be there when I get there. It wouldn't make any difference what part of the States she'd be in. I'd go to her even if I used up my whole furlough doing it.

We came quite far south. We were off the coast of Africa. Yesterday I saw sea gulls and I don't think any were following the ships.

March 11, 1945

The ocean is as smooth as glass today. (Sunday) Although I was working, I got time off to go to Mass in the officers' lounge. This is our fourteenth day on the ship. We're supposed to be in New York sometime tomorrow. We're supposed to get a physical check up sometime today (to see if we're still warm).

March 12, 1945

After fifteen days and nights on the boat, we finally pulled into New York today.

There was the Statue of Liberty waiting for us.

Figure 16. Marcella and John Briol. (Courtesy Marcella Briol)

EPILOGUE

John Briol and Marcella were married, and at the end of World War II he doffed his uniform and returned to his home in Freeport, Minnesota. There he joined his father in the blacksmithing business. He and Marcella had two daughters and a son. After serious illnesses dating back to his war time service, John died in 1972. Lauren Spleth died in 1984, survived by his wife, Rita, two daughters and a grandson. The rest of the crew are still living.

The other crew members also returned to civilian pursuits. John Welch and his wife, Alberta, met in college, and were married in 1948. They graduated together in 1950, with a son nearly a year old, and later adopted a girl and a boy. John was recalled to active duty for the Korean War in 1951, and completed a military career, retiring to form his own aviation business in 1970.

Karl Lambertson did survive being shot down. His experiences as a Prisoner of War paralleled those of other airmen in similar circumstances. His account follows:

We were shot down over Munster on January 22, 1945, and I believe that was our third target. We did not drop our bombs on our primary or secondary target, and we encountered flak on all our bomb runs. We were flying at 23,000 elevation. It was my 23rd mission.

The plane received a direct hit in the bomb bay, with a full load of bombs. The engineer, who planned to jump from the bomb bay, said it was a mess, with bombs hanging every which way. We went into a dive and were pinned to our positions for a few moments, until the pilots dropped the flaps to pull the nose up. The flaps were the only controls operable. The two pilots rode the plane down to about 7,000 elevation and bailed out when it was evident they were not headed westerly toward friendly lines.

All crew members survived. Harry Jolly was the radio operator, Frank Conti the engineer, Harley Ernst, the ball turret gunner, and myself in the waist position.

I jumped first and it must have been high, because it took forever to reach ground. After falling free and before pulling the chute, I was falling flat on my back, with my feet flopping out in front, and I had to turn my head sidewise to see the ground. Apparently how you hold your arms determines whether you fall free, feet first. I was directly over the city of Munster, and for some reason I pulled the two back shrouds and it carried me a considerable distance from the city to an open field. The only problem was deciding which side of a fence to hit, then all of a sudden the ground appeared to come and hit me.

The radio operator jumped after me, and I remember seeing his chute high above me. He had the presence of mind to eat his candy bar while parachuting. He landed on a church steeple in the rubble of Munster. The copilot hid out for about half an hour, until a rifle shot convinced him to come out with hands up.

Harry Jolly and I were interrogated somewhere in Munster, called Chicago gangsters and swine, then marched through Munster to an automobile that took us to a Luftwaffe base not far from the city. The crew was reunited at this base, and conditions were tolerable.

After a few days at the Luftwaffe base, we had a harrowing train ride to solitary confinement near Frankfurt. Interrogation was simple for me, but apparently the officers with rank had it much rougher. A cell with a frosted glass window, a thin blanket, a straw mattress, a cup and a tiny electric heater made for a dismal scene on cold January days. The guards walking up and down the hall turning those heaters off is an event never to be forgotten. At night our shoes were placed outside our door.

Next came a train ride to Wetzlar, where conditions were not too bad, and Red Cross parcels went to one central kitchen. At Wetzlar we received an overcoat, Army issue, shoes, five razor blades and little else in material goods.

The worst train ride was from Wetzlar to Nurenberg, cooped up, ten men to a compartment, for four or five days, and no sanitary conditions. The P-51's came down on our train, but did not fire on our car that was labeled POW's. On a later trip, Frank Conti picked up a .50 caliber slug (hole) through the collar of his overcoat when fighters fired on their box car.

Nurenberg was pretty tough, meager rations, fleas (until we received DDT in one bunch of Red Cross parcels), and

British bombers hitting the rail yards on night missions. From Nurenberg to Moosburg we marched. (7,000+ men). On this march I met the pilot, Jellinek, again, who related his experiences.

Except for the first two days, the march was leisurely from farm community to farm community. Swiss drivers drove three Red Cross trucks, distributed Red Cross parcels and transported those unable to walk, (and the few healthy "goldbricks"). One time I held the rifle of a German guard while he played Beer Barrel Polka. Also one time a German woman filled my bowl with potatoes when I asked for some salt. The news of Roosevelt's death came from a radio in one of the farm houses.

Conditions at Moosburg were crowded, with every nationality represented. Liberation was reasonably quiet until three S. S. troopers opened fire on persons outside their barracks.

Figure 17. Lauren M. Spleth on a Glatton Runway, thirty years later.
(Rita Spleth)

NOTES FROM BERLIN

Various members of Spleth's crew expressed their distress at dropping bombs on people in the cities they bombed, and wondered what terrible things must be happening on the ground. Through a friend who grew up in Berlin, but was not there during the later part of the war, contact was made with two ladies who were there for the worst of the bombing. I asked them specifically about February 3, 1945. Their accounts follow.

Ruth E. Zamphiroff:

I was born and raised in Berlin---in the part that later became the American Sector of Berlin; I lived and worked in Berlin during the war years. In 1945 I was 23 years old and one can say that the war stole (from) us "our youth".

I don't really remember February 3rd, 1945 in particular, but it was a day like many others during the last weeks, months, years! In these terrible months of day and night bombing, life in Berlin had to go on. People had become hardened to the dangers of war---just another air raid, we said!---How many had there been during the last two years? No rest for the weary. But with all the outward "stiff upper lip", one does not forget the anxiety, worries and just plain fear: Will my family, my friends and I still be alive tomorrow? Will I be dead or injured? Will I still have a roof over my head? When you are young, you are quite fearless and can manage somehow, but older people who realized what would happen couldn't cope as well.

We were always ready with our little "air raid valise", containing "precious" items....documents, family photos, an extra pair of shoes, a piece of dress material. At night raids we took our valise down to the cellar and during the day it travelled with us to our office.

I was working at that time in mid-city--near Anhalter Bahnhof, a railroad station for travelling West--with a battery and accumulator company; at least we were never without flash lights and batteries, most important in days when electricity went off.

While working, we listened to the radio and when the regular program was replaced by the tic tic tic of the "Drahtfunk"

(Emergenct Alert) we knew--even before the official air raid sirens were sounded---we knew, another air raid on Berlin; get ready to go around the corner into one of the huge bunkers; at least there we were safe, but worrying about our mother, father, etc. When we came out of the bunker....there was an inferno: houses burning, bombs still exploding, bomb craters in the streets, building complexes completely erased....a terrible sight.

Usually after an air raid public transportation was not working and we had to walk home through "fire storms", injured people, others trying to save some of their belongings from a burning or bombed out house....Fire Departments unable to cope with this inferno. On our way home, always the worry what will we find at home, or don't we have a home any more?

What other thoughts did we have during those days?: When will it be over?! One way or another! By that time hardly anybody believed in a German victory---except maybe some fanatic Nazis, and they must have had their doubts by then. What made you feel miserable was the sight of the down-trodden soldiers who had come to Berlin from the Eastern front; what was their fate....where were they being sent next? To their death for a hopeless cause? The thought that all these enormous sacrifices in human lives and properties should have been for nought, made people fight on and continue to suffer.

Naturally people were cursing the planes that bombed us, seeing the damage and misery that these air raids caused, but I cannot say that all people hated the bombers....We realized this is war and our irresponsible Government should have waved the white flag of surrender before so many human beings were killed and cities destroyed. One can assume that many of the bomber crews dreaded these missions as well.

In any case, at this time there was another fear. The Russians were too close to Berlin! We were hoping that the Americans and British troops would arrive first in Berlin--- unfortunately, that did not happen and we paid dearly.

Berlin had become a battered city, but the spirit of the Berliners was never destroyed.

Eva-Maria Lewis-Reucke:

(She wrote a letter to send her account; excerpts from the letter follow:

206

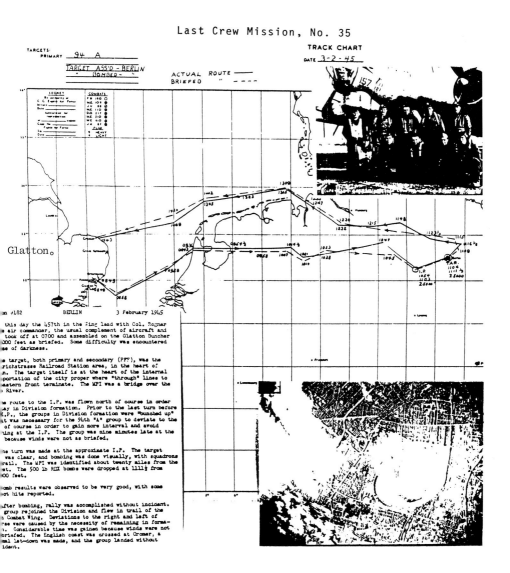

Figure 18. Excerpt of Mission Report, 457th Bomb Group
Mission to Berlin on February 3, 1945. (U.S. Army)

"I...sat down and, best as I could, tried to recapitulate the events on that day....Looking back now, I did not suffer any injury; I was separated from people I loved, I lost some. Other people were left blind or crippled, I was lucky. It was not for my "suffering" that I discarded the story from my mind, but for the whole meaning of "war" as such. But, much as I try, I cannot forget it anyway, and time and again, memories keep popping up in my mind. Oftentimes, when there was an intermission in raids and they were not directly over us, we would stand in the street and share a cigarette, and when looking at those airplanes it occurred to me that there were people up there who had someone trembling for them at home. I felt no hatred, I just wished they would go away...

"Please, use whatever you deem important enough and strike whatever you wish. It certainly is no literary masterpiece, but came from my heart's memory.")

The morning of February 3, 1945, was cold, clear with blue skies, not a cloud in sight. We had the radio going all day as programs were immediately interrupted as soon as plane squadrons were sighted, and we were told how large it was and where it was - probably - headed. On clear days, targets were (more easily) visible, of course. When (the) air raid (warning) was given, we went to the shelter like we had done so many times before. After so many air raids on Berlin, some of which we didn't even feel because of the size of the city, one grew a bit numb, but still alert enough to grab the ever ready suitcase, some food, and always knowing this could be "it". So many had already died, everywhere, everywhere....

At that time I lived more on the outskirts of Berlin, not too far from the "Green Woods" - Gruenewald - , which also had been hit before, and since this particular raid was directed at the old city center where there was some industry left, we did not feel anything of that raid; no howling of the bombs as before, no trembling of the ground, no lights flickering; it was strange, as they had announced a large amount of planes. We joked in the shelter about Goering, who had said that "Meyer shall be his name if ever a foreign airplane enters the territory of the Reich". And then - I do not remember how long it lasted - it was over.

But when we came upstairs again, expecting clear air

and sunshine, we were confronted with skies all covered with a yellow-like fog in which smaller and larger pieces of scorched or burnt paper were flying very slowly. I will never forget this impression, it was like an aftermath of the apocalypse, it was like the breath of death went through the streets with these black pieces of paper moving without a breeze present. It was eerie like from another bad world I had never seen. But we didn't give ourselves time to think, I got ready to try and get into the central section of the city, which was the core of it, after we learned that that was where the raid had taken place. I went to look for my father, who was at the plant, in the office as usual.

At first, I could still use the city railway, but as we approached the city center we had to get out and walk. It would not have been too far to walk, maybe an hour or so, but the entire environment was beyond recognition. Of course, there were no street signs and the streets themselves could not be identified as everything was like upside down. Everywhere I turned, there were sky high rubbles of stone and tile, some house fronts still standing, dangerous to walk past, as they could collapse any second. People were running around, some pulling little carts, with their belongings, behind them; the odor of burnt wood, mixed with wet chalk from broken water pipes, smoke, smoke, and total destruction.

Amazingly, in between, here and there, stood a house unscathed, but of course with a lot of holes in it. I found people shoveling for friends or relatives buried under the mountains of tiles and stones; men from the "Katastrophen-Einsatz", (emergency team) in white overalls were working like mad, sweat streaming down their faces in spite of the cold. Some were left from the night raid before, stretched out on a section of sidewalk, sound asleep from over exhaustion. I took all these impressions in wthout knowing much of it, as I was still getting more and more panicky to find my Dad. It took me at least two hours before I could find a turn and another, and then back again to another, to get to where the factory, which my great grandfather had established in the so-called "founder-years", the 1880's or '90's, once stood. It was no more, like so many others.

In the midst of people moving about senselessly, workers, employees, I saw the company driver and yelled at him to ask if he had seen my father. He yelled back,

"He's o. k. I'll get him".

A little later my Dad came out. I hardly recognized him. His eyes had an expression I had never seen before in this rather peaceful man, like he had seen death, and he probably had. There had been full hits on entire blocks. I knew only too well what he had been through, as we had gone through the same experience two years earlier when we lost our home.

Then we had sat in the dark shelter, (lights had gone out), and counted the hits - one - two - three - four. That had been at night, and the firestorm afterward I shall never forget. I had never encountered the force of fire before to that extent.

Now I was so glad to see him alive. Apparently no one there had been injured, but there were many people dead in the streets farther away. The street ended onto a round square with St. Michael's church in the middle.

(The church was cut in two and stayed that way all through the 40 years of German "Democratic" government in the "East", and only now, 1993, are they beginning to restore it.)

The entire block was gone on both sides. I urged Dad to come with me but he said he had to look after things there, see what could be salvaged. But as it turned out, there was nothing left to salvage, all the machinery was destroyed - as everywhere, everywhere....

So I walked back the long way, hoping to get home before another raid came. I found more people walking, stumbling, climbing, their faces tired, sometimes in tears. It is hard to describe the utter hopelessness, helplessness and hence despair when in an environment of total destruction.

I thought of so many other cities in other countries which had been destroyed, the many people who were killed for no good reason at all. I don't know how many times I asked this within myself, like so many of my friends and millions of other people in other countries,

"How much longer, how much more can anybody endure?"

There is always an end, finally, but the time it takes sometimes is so very hard. There were many air raids in Berlin, lighter ones, heavier ones, but this particular one will always stick in my mind. I can never ever forget the awesome cruelty of war and its violence.

210

GLOSSARY

A-Channel - First of four frequencies (A, B, C, and D) set by installing selected crystals in the Very High Frequency (VHF) radio, changed each day for communications security.

Bandits - enemy fighter aircraft.

Carbohydrate Ration - a small box of very hard candy, developed by the British, noted for high calorie content, but not for flavor.

CBI - China-Burma-India war theater

Channel - the body of water separating Southern England from France; name was used by airmen to refer also to the North Sea between England and the Netherlands.

Chute - Parachute; also a flat tube leading from inside the airplane out into the slipstream for dispensing chaff (the radar reflective strips used to confuse ground defenses).

Class A's - Uniform with blouse (coat) and tie.

Cone of Silence - the small area over a Radio Range navigation station where there is no aural reception.

Contrail - condensation trailing behind a petroleum burning engine, formed from the water vapor produced by oxidation of the hydrogen in the fuel.

CQ - Charge of Quarters, the military person who mans the telephones and takes care of other business of a military unit during non-duty hours.

DFC - Distinguished Flying Cross, a medal awarded for outstanding performance in combat flying.

Division - One of three Heavy Bombardment Divisions in the

Eighth Air Force. There were three Groups per Wing, three Wings per Division.

DR - dead reckoning; navigation using heading, airspeed and estimated or known wind to compute present and future position.

Eighty-eights (88's) - German 88 millimeter cannon (or artillery shells) used for anti-aircraft defense.

Engine Numbers (1, 2, 3, 4,) - identifying engine position on the airplane, counting from left to right, looking forward.

ETO - European Theater of Operations, World War II.

Fatigues - work uniform.

Feather - mechanically (hydraulically) position propeller blades parallel to the airflow past the airplane, to minimize aerodynamic drag when engine rotation is stopped.
To shut down an engine by feathering its propeller.

Flak - anti-aircraft artillery shells.

Flak Shack - restful, peaceful place, usually a large country home, to which combat flight crew members were sent for rest and relaxation when about half way through a combat tour.

Flying blind - flight and control of the airplane when unable to see the ground or horizon, usually due to weather phenomena, solely by reference to the flight instruments.

G-box - a radio receiver using the signals transmitted by paired ground radio stations, to determine flight position on associated charts.

GI - Government Issue; Serviceman.

GI's - Uniform; Diarrhea.

GMT - Greenwich Mean Time, the time at zero degrees longitude, determined by the Greenwich Astronomical Observatory in London

Guns - aircraft machine guns or cannon; anti-aircraft weapons defending specific targets.

Inches (Hg.) - the pressure of the air inside the intake manifold of an engine, measured by the height of a column of mercury (Hg) the pressure would support against a vacuum. Standard atmospheric pressure at sea level is 29.92 inches Hg.

I. P. - Initial Point, the ground point over which the navigator directs the airplane to align it with the target.

K. P. - Kitchen Police - kitchen work detail.

Kilroy - cartoon character always appearing in prominent spots, with caption "Kilroy was here".

Lancaster - a large four engine British bomber.

Mae West - an inflatable life vest, named in honor (?) of the movie actress for the way it bulges in front.

Manifold pressure - a measure of power output of a reciprocating engine, based on pressure inside the air intake manifold (See Inches Hg. above.) Read on a dial on the instrument panel. Maximum reading in the B-17 is 46" (inches) at 2500 RPM, less at lower RPM. (See RPM below).

OD - Olive Drab color, standard color for all dyed or painted U. S. Army issued items in World War II.

OLC - Oak Leaf Cluster; a small bronze oak leaf mounted on a ribbon accompanying a medal, to show that the award has been given again. A silver OLC is equivalent to five bronze OLC's. Crew members who finished 35 missions wore the Air Medal ribbon with two bronze OLC's and a silver OLC.

Oxygen check - a check of the functioning of one's oxygen flow regulator, mask and hose connections, and pressure of the oxygen available. At high altitude the check is initiated by a designated crew member every five minutes, with each other member responding in turn. Lack of response is a danger signal.

P. X. - Post Exchange; Army store that sells miscellaneous items, such as toiletries, cigarettes, candy, stationery and magazines to servicemen.

Peeled off - turned steeply out of formation, as for landing.

Radio Range Station - a ground radio transmitting station, broadcasting signals in a specific geographical pattern, which can be used for aerial navigation.

RPM - revolutions per minute of the engine; 2500 was maximum RPM on the B-17. The combination of MP and RPM indicated power output.

Runaway - loss of control of speed of rotation of a propeller.

Sack - slang term meaning bed.

Sad Sack - sad looking friend of cartoon character, Kilroy.

Short arm - Doctor's inspection of penis, looking for symptoms of venereal disease.

Siegfried line - the fortified line along the boundary of Germany with its Western neighbors.

Slipstream - flow of air past the airplane in flight.

Socked in - weather so thick with fog, clouds, rain, snow and/or other obstruction to vision that visual flying is not possible.

SOP - Standard Operating Procedure, the way of doing things or responding to specific events, established ahead of time.

Square eggs - powdered eggs, sometimes with powdered milk, mixed with water, cooked on large baking sheets, then cut into squares for serving.

Stirling - a large British four engine bomber.

Strafe - fire airborne automatic weapons at ground targets.

Supercharger - a device for pressurizing the air being supplied to a reciprocating engine to increase power output, essential to maintain power at the reduced atmospheric pressure of high altitude.

Synthetic Oil Refinery - a large industrial facility for converting coal into liquid fuels and lubricants, as substitutes for petroleum products.

Tannoy - British public address system

Tokyo Tanks - extended range fuel tanks installed outboard of the standard tanks in the wings, intended (?) to make possible (?) the bombing of Tokyo.

Touch and go - follow a landing by taking off again without having come to a full stop.

Turbo - a supercharger powered by the exhaust gases of its engine turning a gas turbine in the exhaust system.

VD - venereal disease.

VHF - Very High Frequency radio; line of sight communication with little or no static. Frequency is crystal controlled.

Viaticum - Holy Communion for a person whose life is in danger.

Waist - the portion of the airplane fuselage between the wings and the tail surfaces (large bombers).

Walls of the Missing - Each U. S. Military Cemetery in Europe has a wall listing the names and assigned units of men missing in action in the area, of whom no identifiable remains have ever been found.

Wing de-icers - Rubber bladders covering the leading edges of the wings and horizontal and vertical stabilizers. They can be inflated to break off ice that has accumulated on the leading edges, allowing most of the ice to be blown away in the slipstream.

Zuider Zee - the large area of shallow water surrounded mostly by land, in the Netherlands.